GROWING A GREENER TOMORROW

A GUIDE TO TREE PLANTING & CONSERVATION

DR. MINAKSHI BANSAL

DEDICATION

This book is dedicated to all the women who have nurtured the earth, planted seeds of hope, and paved the way for a more sustainable future. Your wisdom, strength, and unwavering commitment to the environment inspire us all. May this book serve as a tribute to your legacy and empower future generations of women to continue your vital work.

ppp

Contents

Prayer   *ix*

About The Author   *xi*

Preface   *xv*

1. Dig In, Branch Out: A Woman's Guide To Growing A Greener 1
World.

Part 1

2. From Acorn To Oak: Nurturing Nature, One Tree At A Time.   7

Part 2

3. The Woman's Way To A Leafy Legacy: Planting Trees For A   13
Thriving Tomorrow.

Part 3

4. Rooted In Hope: A Practical Guide To Tree Planting & Care.   19

Part 4

5. Bloom Where You're Planted: Cultivating Change Through   25
Trees.

Part 5

6. The Tree Lady's Handbook: Everything You Need To Know   31
To Get Growing.

Part 6

7. Growing Green With Grace: A Female-Focused Approach To   39
Conservation.

Part 7

8. A Seed Of Change: Empowering Women To Plant The Future. 45

Part 8

9. She Who Plants A Tree, Plants Hope: A Guide To Reforesting 51
Our Planet.

Contents

Part 9

10. The Art Of Arboriculture: A Woman's Touch In Tree   57

    Cultivation.

Part 10

11. Leave A Legacy In Leaves: A Practical Guide To Planting   63

    Trees.

Part 11

12. A Woman's Guide To Forestry: Empowering The Next   69

    Generation Of Tree Huggers.

Part 12

13. From Sapling To Success: A Step-by-Step Guide To Tree   75

    Planting.

Part 13

14. Cultivating Connections: How Trees Can Heal And Transform. 81

Part 14

15. Trees As Teachers: Lessons In Sustainability From Nature.   87

Part 15

16. The Green Goddess Guide: Unleashing Your Inner Arborist.   93

Part 16

17. Planting Seeds Of Empowerment: Women Leading The Way   99

    In Conservation.

Part 17

18. The Joy Of Growing: A Celebration Of Trees And The Women 105

    Who Love Them.

Part 18

19. A Woman's Roots Run Deep: Finding Strength And Resilience 111

Contents

Through Nature.

Part 19

20. Growing Together: Building Community Through Trees.   117

Part 20

21. The Canopy Of Change: How Trees Can Revitalize Our   123

Planet.

Part 21

22. A Woman's Touch: Nurturing Nature For A Sustainable   129

Future.

Part 22

23. A Symphony Of Green: Creating Harmony Through Tree   135

Planting.

Part 23

24. SUMMARY   141

Citation and References   145

Other Books of the Author   147

CONTACT   153

Prayer

"Om Bhadram Karnebhih Shrinuyama Devah

Bhadram Pashyemakshabhiryajatrah

Sthirairangais Tushtuvamsastanubhih

Vyashema Devahitam Yadayuh

Svasti Na Indro Vriddhashravah

Svasti Nah Pusha Vishwavedah

Svasti Nastarkshyo Arishtanemih

Svasti No Brihaspatir Dadhatu

Om Shantih Shantih Shantih"

This mantra is a prayer for universal well-being, invoking the blessings of various deities for protection, health, and happiness. It emphasizes the importance of experiencing the auspicious through all senses and living a life aligned with divine purpose. The repetition of "Shantih" at the end signifies a deep desire for peace in the individual, the environment, and the universe at large. This mantra is often recited as a prayer for peace, prosperity, and the physical and spiritual well-being of all beings.

༄༄༄

About The Author

This book represents the culmination of extensive research and meticulous analysis, incorporating a diverse range of sources, including numerous books, scholarly studies, and personal experiences. Additionally, I have scoured various websites to gather relevant information and data essential for the compilation of this work. I have taken every precaution to ensure the accuracy of the information presented and have diligently cited all sources to acknowledge their contributions.

From her earliest days, Minakshi was distinguished by an insatiable appetite for reading. Her literary universe was inhabited by characters and narratives that spanned ethical tales, motivational and inspirational stories, and the mythic parables imbued with life lessons. This voracious reading habit was not merely for personal edification but was driven by a desire to distill and disseminate the essence of these narratives to foster the development of students and peers alike. She was particularly captivated by the lives and teachings of historical figures and spiritual leaders such as Adi Shankaracharya, Swami Vivekananda, Dr. APJ Abdul Kalam, Mahamana Pandit Madan Mohan Malviya, Mahatma Gandhi, Sardar Vallabhai Patel, and Vinoba Bhave, among others. Their philosophies and life stories fueled her ambition to embody their ideals of resilience, selflessness, and relentless pursuit of knowledge.

Dr. Minakshi's academic and practical engagement with psychology has been equally noteworthy. As a research scholar, her focus has been on exploring the intricate tapestry of the human psyche, aiming to unlock the potential for psychological well-being and societal harmony. Her scholarly work is complemented by her active involvement in social work, where she employs her academic insights to make tangible differences in the lives of the underprivileged. Her endeavours in social work are characterized by an innovative approach that combines traditional wisdom with contemporary psychological practices to address the multifaceted challenges faced by these communities.

Her artistic talents, another facet of her diverse capabilities, are not merely a personal passion but also serve as a medium through which she communicates and connects with others. Her art, rich in symbolism and emotional depth, reflects her philosophical inquiries and social concerns, offering viewers a glimpse into the breadth of her intellect and the depth of her compassion.

In addition to her contributions to the arts and social sciences, Dr. Minakshi has embraced the healing arts of Pranic Healing, mastering the techniques developed by Master Choa Kok Sui. This practice, which focuses on the manipulation of Prana or life energy to heal the body and aura, has been both a personal journey of discovery and a means through which she extends her healing touch to others. Her proficiency in Pranic Healing is complemented by her advocacy and teaching of various forms of meditation aimed at rejuvenation, personal betterment, and the cultivation of harmony within individuals and communities alike.

Dr. Minakshi's life is a narrative of relentless pursuit, not just of personal achievement but of the upliftment and empowerment of society at large. Her diverse interests and talents—spanning the arts, literature, psychology, and the healing practices—converge on a singular path of service. She embodies the spirit of the luminaries who inspired her, channelling their legacy through her actions and teachings. Through her books, art, and social initiatives, she continues to inspire a new generation to embark on their own journeys of self-discovery, resilience, and altruism.

Her commitment to social betterment, particularly her focus on uplifting underprivileged children, reflects a deep understanding of the transformative potential of education and personal development. By integrating her knowledge of psychology, her artistic sensibilities, and her healing practices, Dr. Bansal has developed a holistic approach to social work that addresses both the immediate needs and the long-term well-being of the communities she serves.

As an author, Dr. Minakshi's writings offer a blend of inspirational insights, practical wisdom, and reflective contemplations drawn from her extensive reading and life experiences. Her books serve as a guide for those seeking to navigate the complexities of life with grace, resilience, and purpose. Through her narratives, she extends an invitation to her readers to explore the depths of their own potential and to contribute meaningfully to the collective well-being of society.

In Dr. Minakshi Bansal, we find a remarkable synthesis of the artist, the scholar, the healer, and the social activist. Her life's work stands as a beacon of hope and a source of inspiration for individuals seeking to make a difference in the world. Her story is a compelling reminder of the power of individual action, rooted in compassion and driven by a profound commitment to the betterment of humanity. Dr. Minakshi's legacy is not just in the tangible outcomes of her efforts but in the enduring spirit of inquiry, empathy, and service that she embodies.

ᏆᏆᏆ

Preface

In a world grappling with the urgent need for environmental healing and sustainability, I invite you to embark on a journey of growth, renewal, and empowerment. This book is not merely a guide to planting trees; it is a celebration of the profound connection between women and the natural world, a testament to our innate ability to nurture, cultivate, and restore.

As a woman, I have always been drawn to the quiet strength and resilience of trees. Their roots anchor them to the earth, their branches reach towards the sky, and their leaves whisper secrets to the wind. They are the silent witnesses to the passage of time, the keepers of our planet's history, and the providers of life-giving oxygen, food, and shelter.

In my own life, trees have been a source of solace, inspiration, and empowerment. They have taught me valuable lessons about patience, perseverance, and the interconnectedness of all living things. They have shown me that even the smallest actions, like planting a seed, can have a profound impact on the world around us.

Inspired by my own experiences and the stories of countless women who have dedicated their lives to the care and preservation of trees, I have created this book as a resource and a call to action. In this book, you will find practical advice on how to select, plant, and care for trees, as well as insights into the ecological, social, and personal benefits of tree planting.

But this book is more than just a how-to guide. It is a celebration of the feminine spirit of nurturing and caregiving, a recognition of the unique role that women play in environmental stewardship. Throughout history, women have been the keepers of traditional ecological knowledge, the healers of the land, and the protectors of biodiversity. In this book, we honor this legacy and invite women to embrace their role as leaders in the movement for a more sustainable future.

We will explore the diverse ways in which women are contributing to tree planting and conservation efforts around the world, from grassroots initiatives to global campaigns. We will hear from women who have dedicated their lives to the care of trees, from foresters and arborists to activists and educators. Their stories will inspire and empower us to take action in our own communities.

We will also delve into the science of trees, exploring their complex biology, their ecological functions, and their role in mitigating climate change. We will learn about the different types of trees, the best practices for planting and care, and the challenges they face in a changing world. This knowledge will empower us to make informed decisions about tree planting and to become advocates for their protection.

This book is not just for women, but for anyone who loves trees and cares about the future of our planet. It is an invitation to connect with nature, to learn from its wisdom, and to take action to create a more sustainable and equitable world. By planting trees, we are not only investing in the health of our planet but also in the well-being of future generations.

Dr. Minakshi Bansal
Social Activist
Ahmedabad, Gujarat, Bharat

༜༜༜

ONE

DIG IN, BRANCH OUT: A WOMAN'S GUIDE TO GROWING A GREENER WORLD.

The rustle of leaves, the dappled sunlight filtering through a canopy of green, the sweet scent of blossoms carried on a gentle breeze—these are the gifts of trees, the silent sentinels that have watched over our planet for millennia. They provide us with oxygen, shade, and beauty, and they offer a haven for countless creatures. Yet, in our modern world, we often take these arboreal wonders for granted, forgetting their vital role in maintaining the delicate balance of our ecosystem.

This is where we, the women of the world, step in. We, who nurture and care, who cultivate and create, have a unique connection to the natural world. We understand the importance of planting seeds, both literally and figuratively, and we know that the choices we make today will shape the world our children inherit. This guide is a call to action, an invitation to embrace your inner arborist, to dig in and branch out, to become a champion for trees and a guardian of our planet's future.

Why trees, you might ask? Why not focus on recycling, reducing plastic waste, or conserving water? While all of these are important environmental initiatives, trees offer a myriad of benefits that extend far beyond their aesthetic appeal. They act as natural air purifiers, absorbing carbon dioxide and releasing oxygen, thus mitigating the effects of climate change. They provide habitat for birds, insects, and other wildlife, contributing to biodiversity and ecological resilience. They help to prevent soil erosion, protect water sources, and even reduce noise pollution.

Furthermore, planting trees is a tangible, hands-on way to make a difference. It's an act of hope, a testament to our belief in the future. It's a way to connect with nature, to find solace in the soil, and to leave a lasting legacy for generations to come. And while men have traditionally dominated the fields of forestry and conservation, women are increasingly taking the lead in these areas, bringing their unique perspectives and skills to the table.

So, where do you start? The first step is to educate yourself. Learn about the different types of trees that thrive in your climate, the best practices for planting and caring for them, and the potential challenges you might encounter. There are countless resources available, from books and websites to local nurseries and arboreta. Don't be afraid to ask questions, seek advice, and learn from those who have more experience.

Once you've done your research, it's time to choose your trees. Consider the size and shape of your yard, the amount of sunlight and water available, and the purpose of your planting. Are you looking to create a windbreak, provide shade, attract wildlife, or simply add beauty to your landscape? Each tree has its own unique characteristics, so take your time and select the ones that best suit your needs and preferences.

The next step is to prepare the planting site. This involves digging a hole that is twice as wide as the tree's root ball and just as deep. Loosen the soil at the bottom of the hole and add compost or other organic matter to improve drainage and fertility. Gently remove the tree from its container, being careful not to damage the roots, and place it in the hole. Fill the hole with soil, tamping it down gently to eliminate air pockets. Water the tree thoroughly and add a layer of mulch around the base to help retain moisture and suppress weeds.

After planting, your tree will need ongoing care and attention. Water it regularly, especially during dry spells, and fertilize it according to the recommendations for your particular species. Prune it to remove dead or diseased branches and to shape its growth. Protect it from pests and diseases by monitoring it closely and taking action if necessary.

But tree planting isn't just about individual action. It's about building community, fostering collaboration, and empowering women to take the lead in environmental stewardship. Join a local tree planting organization, volunteer at a community garden, or start your own initiative. Encourage your friends, family, and neighbors to get involved, and share your knowledge and passion with others.

Remember, every tree you plant is a gift to the future, a symbol of hope and resilience. It's a testament to the power of women to create positive change and a reminder that we are all connected to the natural world. So, dig in, branch out, and let your roots run deep. Together, we can grow a greener tomorrow.

ᗡᗡᗡ

"A woman's hands, like the earth, hold the power to nurture life. Planting a tree is a testament to this power, a gift to the future, and a legacy etched in leaves."

TWO

FROM ACORN TO OAK: NURTURING NATURE, ONE TREE AT A TIME.

An acorn, small and seemingly insignificant, holds within it the promise of a mighty oak, a testament to the incredible power of nature to transform the humble into the extraordinary. It is a symbol of potential, of resilience, and of the enduring cycle of life, death, and renewal. This journey from acorn to oak mirrors our own human journey, a reminder that even the smallest actions can have a profound impact on the world around us.

As women, we are intimately connected to this cycle of growth and transformation. We nurture and care for our families, our communities, and our planet, planting seeds of hope and cultivating a brighter future. We understand that every tree, every plant, every living creature plays a vital role in the intricate web of life. And we recognize that by nurturing nature, we are in turn nurturing ourselves, our children, and the generations to come.

The story of the oak tree begins with a single acorn, a tiny seed packed with nutrients and genetic information. This acorn falls to the ground, where it may lie dormant for months or even years, waiting for the right conditions to germinate. When the time is right, it sends down a taproot, anchoring itself to the earth and drawing up water and nutrients. A shoot emerges, reaching towards the sun, and soon tiny leaves unfurl, beginning the process of photosynthesis.

The young sapling faces numerous challenges in its early years. It must compete with other plants for sunlight and water, withstand the ravages of wind and rain, and fend off hungry herbivores. Yet, with each passing season, it grows stronger and taller, its roots delving deeper into the soil, its branches reaching higher towards the sky. Over time, it becomes a majestic oak, a symbol of strength, longevity, and resilience.

The oak provides a wealth of benefits to the ecosystem. Its leaves produce oxygen, its roots prevent soil erosion, its branches offer shelter to birds and other wildlife, and its acorns provide food for countless creatures. It is a keystone species, a vital component of the forest community, supporting a diverse array of plant and animal life.

Just as the oak tree nurtures the ecosystem, so too do women nurture the world around them. We plant gardens, care for animals, educate children, and advocate for environmental protection. We are the keepers of traditional knowledge, the healers of the sick, the nurturers of the young, and the protectors of the vulnerable. We are the backbone of our families, our communities, and our planet.

Planting a tree is a simple yet profound act. It is a gesture of hope, a commitment to the future, and a tangible way to make a difference. It is a way to connect with nature, to honor the earth, and to leave a lasting legacy for generations to come.

As women, we have a unique connection to trees. We are drawn to their beauty, their strength, and their resilience. We see in them a reflection of ourselves, a reminder of our own capacity for growth, transformation, and renewal. We understand that by nurturing trees, we are nurturing ourselves, our children, and the planet we call home.

So, how can you nurture nature, one tree at a time? The first step is to educate yourself. Learn about the different types of trees that thrive in your climate, the best practices for planting and caring for them, and the challenges they face. There are countless resources available, from books and websites to local nurseries and arboreta.

The next step is to choose a tree that resonates with you. Consider the size and shape of your yard, the amount of sunlight and water available, and the purpose of your planting. Are you looking to create a windbreak, provide shade, attract wildlife, or simply add beauty to your landscape? Each tree has its own unique characteristics, so take your time and select the one that speaks to your heart.

Once you've chosen your tree, it's time to plant it. Dig a hole that is twice as wide as the root ball and just as deep. Loosen the soil at the bottom of the hole and add compost or other organic matter to improve drainage and fertility. Gently remove the tree from its container, being careful not to damage the roots, and place it in the hole. Fill the hole with soil, tamping it down gently to eliminate air pockets. Water the tree thoroughly and add a layer of mulch around the base to help retain moisture and suppress weeds.

After planting, your tree will need ongoing care and attention. Water it regularly, especially during dry spells, and fertilize it according to the recommendations for your particular species. Prune it to remove dead or diseased branches and to shape its growth. Protect it from pests and diseases by monitoring it closely and taking action if necessary.

But planting a tree is just the beginning. It's about nurturing it, watching it grow, and celebrating its milestones. It's about sharing your love of trees with others, encouraging them to plant their own, and creating a community of tree lovers. It's about recognizing the interconnectedness of all living things and understanding that by nurturing nature, we are nurturing ourselves.

So, let us embrace the journey from acorn to oak, from seed to sapling to towering giant. Let us nurture nature, one tree at a time, and create a world where both trees and women thrive. Let us remember that even the smallest actions can have a ripple effect, leading to a more beautiful, sustainable, and resilient future for all.

ᗞᗞᗞ

"From tiny acorn to towering oak, a tree's journey mirrors our own. It teaches us patience, resilience, and the unwavering pursuit of growth, even amidst adversity."

THREE

THE WOMAN'S WAY TO A LEAFY LEGACY: PLANTING TREES FOR A THRIVING TOMORROW.

In the tapestry of life, women have always been weavers of dreams, nurturers of growth, and architects of legacy. Our innate ability to foster, cultivate, and sustain has shaped families, communities, and, indeed, the very landscapes we inhabit. Now, more than ever, the world calls for this feminine touch, this intuitive understanding of the delicate balance between humanity and nature. Planting trees, an act as ancient as it is profound, is a woman's way to weave a leafy legacy, a living testament to our commitment to a thriving tomorrow.

For millennia, trees have been revered as symbols of strength, wisdom, and interconnectedness. They are the lungs of our planet, inhaling carbon dioxide and exhaling the life-giving oxygen we breathe. They are the guardians of our soil, preventing erosion and enriching the earth with their fallen leaves and decaying wood. They are the providers of shade, shelter, and sustenance for countless creatures, from the tiniest insects to the mightiest mammals. And they are the silent witnesses to the passage of time, their rings recording the history of our planet and the stories of our lives.

In many cultures, women have a special relationship with trees. We are the gatherers of fruits and nuts, the weavers of baskets and textiles from bark and leaves, the healers who use plant extracts to soothe ailments. We are the storytellers who pass down the lore of the forest, the artists who find inspiration in the intricate patterns of leaves and branches, and the poets who sing of the beauty and mystery of the natural world.

But our connection to trees goes deeper than mere utility or aesthetics. It is a spiritual bond, a recognition of our shared origins and our mutual dependence. When we plant a tree, we are not simply adding another green object to the landscape; we are participating in a sacred act of creation. We are planting a seed of hope, a symbol of our faith in the future, and a living legacy that will outlive us all.

A woman's way to a leafy legacy is not about grand gestures or heroic feats. It is about the small, everyday actions that, when multiplied by millions, can have a transformative impact on the world. It is about planting a tree in your backyard, volunteering at a local park, or supporting organizations that work to conserve forests. It is about teaching your children the importance of trees, sharing your knowledge with your community, and advocating for policies that protect our natural resources.

Planting trees is also a way to empower women and girls. In many parts of the world, women are disproportionately affected by environmental degradation, as they are often responsible for collecting water and firewood, and for growing food for their families. By participating in tree planting and conservation efforts, women can gain valuable skills, earn income, and improve their livelihoods. They can also become leaders in their communities, advocating for sustainable practices and inspiring others to follow their lead.

The benefits of planting trees are not limited to the environment. Studies have shown that spending time in nature can reduce stress, improve mood, and boost creativity. Trees can also help to mitigate the urban heat island effect, reduce noise pollution, and provide habitat for wildlife. In short, planting trees is a win-win for both people and the planet.

As women, we have a unique opportunity to create a leafy legacy that will benefit generations to come. We can plant trees that will provide shade for our children and grandchildren, clean air for our communities, and habitat for wildlife. We can support organizations that are working to restore forests and protect endangered species. We can advocate for policies that promote sustainable forestry and reduce our reliance on fossil fuels. And we can teach our children the importance of respecting and caring for the natural world.

The woman's way to a leafy legacy is not a one-size-fits-all approach. It is a personal journey, a unique expression of our individual values and passions. Some of us may choose to plant trees in our own backyards, while others may volunteer at local parks or arboreta. Some of us may become educators or advocates, while others may support organizations that are working to protect forests around the world.

The important thing is to take action, to find your own way to contribute to the greening of our planet. Whether you plant a single tree or a thousand, your contribution will make a difference. It will be a testament to your love for the earth, your commitment to the future, and your belief in the power of women to create positive change.

❧❧❧

"The forest whispers secrets of sustainability, urging us to live in harmony with nature. Listen closely, for within its depths lies the wisdom we need to heal our planet."

FOUR

ROOTED IN HOPE: A PRACTICAL GUIDE TO TREE PLANTING & CARE.

In a world grappling with environmental challenges, the simple act of planting a tree emerges as a beacon of hope. Rooted in the earth, these arboreal wonders offer a multitude of benefits, from purifying our air and water to providing shelter for wildlife and mitigating the impacts of climate change. "Rooted in Hope" is more than a guide; it's an invitation to participate in a timeless act of nurturing nature, fostering a legacy of verdant beauty and ecological balance for generations to come.

The journey begins with understanding the profound significance of trees in our ecosystem. These silent sentinels are not merely decorative elements in our landscape, but rather vital components of a complex web of life. They absorb carbon dioxide, a major greenhouse gas, and release oxygen, the lifeblood of our planet. Their roots bind the soil, preventing erosion and filtering rainwater, while their branches provide habitat and sustenance for a myriad of creatures. By planting trees, we are not simply adding greenery to our surroundings; we are actively contributing to the health and resilience of our planet.

Choosing the right tree for the right place is the cornerstone of successful tree planting. Different species have varying requirements for sunlight, soil type, and moisture levels. Consider your local climate and the specific characteristics of your planting site. Researching native trees is often the best approach, as they are adapted to the local conditions and tend to thrive with minimal intervention. Consult with local nurseries or arborists for expert advice on selecting trees that will flourish in your area.

Planting a tree is a ritual of hope, a tangible expression of our belief in the future. Start by digging a hole that is twice as wide as the tree's root ball and just as deep. This will allow the roots to spread out and establish themselves firmly in the soil. Gently remove the tree from its container, taking care not to damage the delicate root system. Place the tree in the hole, ensuring that the top of the root ball is level with the surrounding ground. Backfill the hole with soil, tamping it down gently to eliminate air pockets.

Watering is essential for the survival and growth of newly planted trees. During the first few years, regular watering is crucial, especially during dry spells. A slow, deep soak is preferable to frequent, shallow watering, as it encourages the roots to grow deeper into the soil, making the tree more drought-tolerant. Mulching around the base of the tree helps to retain moisture, suppress weeds, and regulate soil temperature.

As your tree matures, pruning becomes an important aspect of care. Pruning helps to shape the tree, remove dead or diseased branches, and improve air circulation. It's best to prune during the dormant season, typically in late winter or early spring, before new growth begins. Always use sharp, clean tools to make clean cuts and avoid damaging the tree.

Trees, like any living organism, are susceptible to pests and diseases. Regular inspection is key to early detection and prompt intervention. Look for signs of insect infestation, such as chewed leaves or discolored foliage. Fungal diseases can manifest as spots, wilting, or cankers on the bark. If you notice any signs of trouble, consult with a local arborist or plant pathologist for diagnosis and treatment options.

Beyond the practical aspects of planting and care, trees have a profound impact on our well-being. Studies have shown that spending time in nature, surrounded by trees, can reduce stress, lower blood pressure, and boost our immune system. Trees also provide a sense of tranquility and connection to the natural world, offering a refuge from the hustle and bustle of modern life.

Planting trees is not only an act of environmental stewardship but also an investment in the future. Trees can increase property values, provide shade and energy savings, and enhance the beauty of our communities. They create a legacy that will be enjoyed for generations to come, a testament to our commitment to a greener and more sustainable world.

"Rooted in Hope" is a call to action, an invitation to embrace the power of trees to transform our lives and our planet. By planting and caring for trees, we are not merely cultivating greenery; we are cultivating hope, resilience, and a profound connection to the natural world. So let us dig in, nurture these arboreal wonders, and watch as they grow, flourish, and inspire us all.

ᗅᗅᗅ

"A woman's roots run deep, intertwined with the very fabric of the earth. In nurturing the soil, we nurture ourselves, finding strength and solace in the embrace of nature."

FIVE

BLOOM WHERE YOU'RE PLANTED: CULTIVATING CHANGE THROUGH TREES.

The adage "bloom where you're planted" carries profound wisdom, urging us to thrive amidst adversity, to make the most of our circumstances, and to find beauty and purpose wherever we may be. When applied to the context of trees and environmental stewardship, this phrase takes on a new dimension, reminding us that even the smallest actions, like planting a tree, can cultivate change and create a flourishing future.

Trees, in their silent strength, embody the essence of this philosophy. They take root in the earth, drawing sustenance from the soil, and reaching towards the sky, transforming sunlight into life-giving energy. They adapt to their environment, weathering storms, droughts, and pests, and yet they continue to grow, to bloom, and to provide for the world around them. They teach us that resilience, adaptability, and perseverance are essential for thriving in an ever-changing world.

The act of planting a tree is a tangible expression of hope, a declaration of our commitment to a better future. It is a way of saying, "I believe in the power of nature to heal and restore, and I am willing to do my part to create a more beautiful and sustainable world." It is a gesture of faith in the next generation, a gift of shade, clean air, and natural beauty that will be enjoyed for years to come.

But the impact of planting trees goes far beyond the individual act. It is a catalyst for change, a ripple effect that spreads throughout the community and beyond. Trees have the power to transform barren landscapes into thriving ecosystems, to mitigate the effects of climate change, to improve air and water quality, and to provide habitat for wildlife. They also have a profound impact on human health and well-being, reducing stress, promoting relaxation, and fostering a sense of connection to nature.

Moreover, planting trees is a community-building activity. It brings people together from all walks of life, united by a common purpose. It fosters collaboration, shared learning, and a sense of collective responsibility for the environment. It empowers individuals to take action, to make a difference, and to be part of something bigger than themselves.

The process of planting a tree is a metaphor for personal growth and transformation. Just as a seed needs the right conditions to germinate and grow, so too do we need nurturing, support, and the right environment to flourish. We must be willing to put down roots, to embrace our unique strengths and weaknesses, and to reach for the light. We must be patient, persistent, and resilient in the face of challenges. And we must be willing to adapt to change and to learn from our mistakes.

The rewards of planting trees are manifold. They provide us with tangible benefits, such as shade, fruit, and wood. They also offer intangible rewards, such as beauty, inspiration, and a sense of peace. But perhaps the most significant reward is the knowledge that we have made a positive contribution to the world, that we have left a legacy that will endure for generations to come.

In a world that often feels overwhelming and chaotic, planting a tree is a simple yet powerful way to make a difference. It is a tangible expression of our values, our hopes, and our dreams. It is a way to connect with nature, to honor the earth, and to create a more beautiful, sustainable, and equitable world.

So, let us all embrace the philosophy of "bloom where you're planted." Let us plant trees in our yards, our communities, and our hearts. Let us nurture them with care and watch them grow, flourish, and inspire us to become better stewards of the earth. And let us remember that even the smallest actions can have a profound impact, that each tree we plant is a seed of hope, a symbol of our commitment to a thriving tomorrow.

❧❧❧

"The canopy of change begins with a single seed.
Each tree we plant is a brushstroke in the
masterpiece of a greener tomorrow."

SIX

THE TREE LADY'S HANDBOOK: EVERYTHING YOU NEED TO KNOW TO GET GROWING.

Welcome, fellow tree enthusiasts, to "The Tree Lady's Handbook," your comprehensive guide to the captivating world of trees! Whether you're a seasoned arborist or a budding green thumb, this handbook is designed to equip you with the knowledge and inspiration needed to cultivate a thriving arboreal haven. Let's embark on this journey together and uncover the secrets of these magnificent living beings that grace our planet.

Understanding the Tree's Essence

Trees, the silent sentinels of nature, are far more than mere ornaments in our landscapes. They are the lifeblood of our ecosystem, providing us with oxygen, purifying our air, and offering shelter to a multitude of creatures. Understanding their fundamental needs is paramount to ensuring their well-being.

Roots: The unsung heroes, roots anchor the tree, absorb water and nutrients, and store energy.

Trunk and Branches: The sturdy framework, supporting the tree's weight and transporting resources.

Leaves: Nature's solar panels, harnessing sunlight for photosynthesis and producing oxygen.

Selecting Your Arboreal Companions

Choosing the right tree is akin to finding a lifelong companion. It's a decision that requires careful consideration of your environment, personal preferences, and long-term goals.

Native vs. Exotic: Native trees are often the best choice, as they're adapted to the local climate and soil conditions.

Size and Shape: Consider the available space and the desired aesthetic impact.

Purpose: Are you seeking shade, privacy, fruit, or ornamental beauty? Each tree offers unique benefits.

Planting with Purpose

Planting a tree is an act of hope and optimism, a gift to future generations. However, proper planting is crucial for the tree's survival and long-term health.

Timing: Spring and fall are generally the best times to plant, as the weather is mild and conducive to root growth.

Site Preparation: Ensure the planting site has well-draining soil, adequate sunlight, and sufficient space for the mature tree.

Planting Technique: Dig a hole twice as wide as the root ball, but no deeper. Gently loosen the roots and place the tree in the hole, backfilling with soil and watering thoroughly.

Nurturing Your Growing Family

Trees, like any living being, require care and attention to thrive. By understanding their needs, you can ensure they reach their full potential.

Watering: Young trees need regular watering, especially during dry periods. As they mature, they become more drought-tolerant.

Fertilizing: A balanced fertilizer can provide essential nutrients, but be cautious not to over-fertilize.

Mulching: A layer of mulch around the base of the tree helps retain moisture, suppress weeds, and regulate soil temperature.

Pruning: Regular pruning removes dead or diseased branches, promotes healthy growth, and enhances the tree's natural shape.

Identifying and Addressing Challenges

Trees, despite their resilience, can face challenges from pests, diseases, and environmental stressors. Early detection and intervention are key to preserving their health.

Pests: Common pests include aphids, borers, and scale insects. Natural remedies like insecticidal soap or neem oil can often be effective.

Diseases: Fungal infections, bacterial diseases, and viruses can affect trees. Proper sanitation and fungicide applications may be necessary.

Environmental Stressors: Drought, extreme temperatures, and pollution can weaken trees. Providing supplemental water and protection can help mitigate these stressors.

The Tree Lady's Wisdom

Beyond the practical aspects of tree care, there's a deeper wisdom to be gleaned from these arboreal companions.

Patience and Perseverance: Trees teach us the importance of patience and perseverance. They grow slowly but steadily, enduring challenges and setbacks along the way.

Interconnectedness: Trees remind us that we are all part of a larger ecosystem, interconnected and interdependent.

Resilience and Renewal: Trees demonstrate remarkable resilience, even in the face of adversity. They can recover from damage, regrow lost branches, and continue to thrive.

Embracing the Tree Lady Spirit

The Tree Lady embodies a spirit of nurturing, respect, and reverence for the natural world. By following her guidance, you too can cultivate this spirit and become an advocate for trees.

Sharing Your Passion: Inspire others to plant and care for trees by sharing your knowledge and enthusiasm.

Supporting Conservation Efforts: Join local tree-planting initiatives or donate to organizations dedicated to protecting forests.

Advocating for Trees: Raise your voice in support of policies that protect trees and promote sustainable forestry practices.

A Growing Legacy

By planting and caring for trees, you are not only creating a greener and more beautiful world, but you are also leaving a lasting legacy for future generations. Your actions today will echo through the ages, as the trees you plant continue to grow, thrive, and provide benefits for centuries to come. So let us embrace the wisdom of the Tree Lady, dig in our heels, and cultivate a future rooted in hope, resilience, and the enduring beauty of trees.

🌳🌳🌳

"Let the rhythm of the seasons guide your hands as you plant. The earth rejoices in the touch of a woman who understands the language of growth."

SEVEN

GROWING GREEN WITH GRACE: A FEMALE-FOCUSED APPROACH TO CONSERVATION.

In the symphony of nature, women have always played a harmonious role, their innate nurturing instincts and intuitive connection to the earth fostering a unique relationship with the environment. "Growing Green with Grace" is an exploration of this female-focused approach to conservation, celebrating the power of feminine energy to cultivate a sustainable and thriving planet.

Throughout history, women have been the custodians of nature's bounty, their roles as gatherers, farmers, and healers inextricably linked to the rhythms of the earth. They possess an intimate knowledge of plants, animals, and the delicate balance of ecosystems, passed down through generations of wisdom and experience. This inherent understanding of the natural world, coupled with a deep sense of empathy and interconnectedness, makes women powerful agents of change in the realm of conservation.

The feminine approach to conservation is characterized by a holistic perspective that recognizes the interconnectedness of all living beings. It values collaboration over competition, emphasizes cooperation over domination, and prioritizes long-term sustainability over short-term gains. It embraces diversity and recognizes the unique contributions that each individual, each species, and each ecosystem can make to the health of the planet.

One of the most powerful expressions of this female-focused approach is the act of planting trees. Trees, as symbols of life, growth, and resilience, resonate deeply with the feminine spirit. They provide nourishment, shelter, and healing, mirroring the nurturing role that women play in their families and communities. By planting trees, women are not only contributing to the restoration of ecosystems, but also fostering a sense of hope and renewal for future generations.

The act of planting a tree is a ritual of connection, a tangible expression of our love for the earth. It involves digging our hands into the soil, feeling the coolness of the earth, and placing a seed in the ground with the intention of nurturing it to life. It is a humbling experience that reminds us of our own place in the grand scheme of things, as well as our responsibility to care for the natural world.

Women-led conservation initiatives are flourishing around the world, demonstrating the power of feminine energy to create positive change. From grassroots movements to global organizations, women are leading the way in protecting forests, restoring degraded lands, and promoting sustainable practices. They are educating their communities, empowering women and girls, and advocating for policies that protect the environment.

In many cultures, women have a deep understanding of the medicinal properties of plants. They have traditionally used herbs, roots, and bark to treat ailments and promote health. This knowledge, often passed down through generations of women, is an invaluable resource for conservation efforts, as it can help to identify and protect plant species with medicinal value.

Women's leadership in conservation is also essential for addressing the social and economic dimensions of environmental issues. Women are often disproportionately affected by environmental degradation, as they are often responsible for collecting water and firewood, and for growing food for their families. By empowering women and girls, conservation initiatives can create a ripple effect of positive change, improving livelihoods, promoting gender equality, and building more resilient communities.

The feminine approach to conservation is not about excluding men or diminishing their contributions. Rather, it is about recognizing the unique strengths that women bring to the table and creating a more inclusive and collaborative approach to environmental stewardship. Men and women working together, each bringing their unique perspectives and skills, can achieve far more than either could alone.

Growing green with grace is a journey of personal and collective transformation. It is about recognizing our interconnectedness with the natural world and taking responsibility for our actions. It is about embracing the feminine qualities of nurturing, collaboration, and intuition, and using them to create a more sustainable and equitable world.

As women, we have a vital role to play in the future of our planet. By planting trees, protecting forests, and promoting sustainable practices, we can create a leafy legacy that will benefit generations to come. We can empower women and girls, build resilient communities, and foster a deeper connection to the natural world.

So let us embrace the power of feminine energy, let us grow green with grace, and let us create a world where both nature and humanity can thrive.

❧❧❧

*"In the heart of every woman lies a Green Goddess,
a protector of the earth and a nurturer of life.
Awaken this spirit and watch your impact
blossom."*

EIGHT

A Seed of Change: Empowering Women to Plant the Future.

In the heart of every seed lies the promise of growth, transformation, and renewal. This metaphor extends far beyond the realm of botany, encapsulating the potential that resides within each individual, particularly women, to cultivate a better future for themselves, their communities, and the planet as a whole. "A Seed of Change: Empowering Women to Plant the Future" is an exploration of this potent concept, highlighting the vital role women play in environmental conservation and sustainable development.

Women have an intrinsic connection to the earth, a relationship that has been nurtured through centuries of agricultural practices, traditional ecological knowledge, and a deep understanding of natural cycles. They are the primary stewards of the land in many communities, responsible for food production, water management, and the preservation of biodiversity. Yet, despite their pivotal role, women often face systemic barriers that limit their access to resources, education, and decision-making power.

Empowering women to plant the future means recognizing and valuing their contributions, providing them with the tools and resources they need to thrive, and amplifying their voices in shaping environmental policies and practices. It involves challenging gender norms and stereotypes that perpetuate inequality, and creating a more inclusive and equitable space for women to lead and innovate.

One of the most powerful ways to empower women in the environmental sphere is through education and training. By equipping women with knowledge about sustainable agriculture, forestry, and resource management, we enable them to become agents of change in their communities. This not only enhances their livelihoods but also strengthens their resilience in the face of climate change and other environmental challenges.

Access to land and resources is another critical aspect of empowering women in environmental conservation. Land ownership provides women with security, autonomy, and the ability to invest in sustainable practices. By ensuring women have secure land tenure and access to credit, we can unlock their full potential as environmental stewards.

Women's leadership in environmental organizations and decision-making bodies is essential for driving meaningful change. When women are involved in shaping environmental policies and programs, they bring unique perspectives and priorities to the table, ensuring that the needs of women and marginalized communities are taken into account. This leads to more effective and equitable solutions that benefit both people and the planet.

The empowerment of women in the environmental field is not only a matter of justice and equality; it is also a strategic imperative.

Studies have shown that when women are empowered, they invest more in their families and communities, leading to improved health, education, and economic outcomes. This, in turn, contributes to greater environmental sustainability, as empowered women are more likely to adopt environmentally friendly practices and advocate for policies that protect the planet.

Women-led conservation initiatives are flourishing around the world, demonstrating the transformative power of female leadership. These initiatives often prioritize community engagement, education, and sustainable livelihoods, creating a ripple effect of positive change that extends far beyond the immediate project goals.

One inspiring example is the Green Belt Movement, founded by Nobel Peace Prize laureate Wangari Maathai. This grassroots organization has empowered millions of women in Kenya and other African countries to plant trees, restore degraded lands, and improve their livelihoods. The Green Belt Movement not only addresses environmental degradation but also empowers women economically and politically, creating a model for sustainable development that is rooted in gender equality.

Another inspiring example is the Women's Earth Alliance, a global organization that supports women-led environmental initiatives around the world. Through training, mentorship, and funding, the Women's Earth Alliance empowers women to become leaders in their communities, tackling issues such as climate change, deforestation, and water scarcity.

These are just a few examples of the countless ways in which women are planting the seeds of change for a more sustainable and equitable future. Their stories remind us that empowering women is not only the right thing to do but also the smart thing to do. By investing in women's leadership and supporting their efforts to protect the environment, we are investing in a future that is healthier, more resilient, and more just for all.

The journey towards a sustainable future is a collective one, and women are at the forefront of this movement. They are the seed planters, the nurturers, the guardians of our planet. By empowering women to plant the future, we are not only creating a more equitable world, but we are also ensuring the health and well-being of our planet for generations to come.

ﭮﭮﭮ

"To plant a tree is to plant hope, to believe in a future where the air is clean, the water is pure, and the earth is teeming with life."

NINE

She Who Plants a Tree, Plants Hope: A Guide to Reforesting Our Planet.

In the intricate tapestry of our planet's ecosystems, trees stand as pillars of life, their roots anchoring the soil, their branches reaching towards the heavens. They are the lungs of our Earth, the providers of shade, sustenance, and shelter for countless creatures. Yet, in our relentless pursuit of progress, we have often overlooked their importance, leading to widespread deforestation and environmental degradation. However, a growing movement, led by women around the world, is rising to the challenge, planting seeds of hope and embarking on a journey to reforest our planet. "She Who Plants a Tree, Plants Hope" is a testament to this empowering movement, a guide to reforestation that celebrates the unique role women play in restoring the balance of nature.

Throughout history, women have shared a profound connection with the natural world. They have been the gatherers of wild foods, the cultivators of crops, and the guardians of traditional ecological knowledge. They have an intimate understanding of the land, its cycles, and the delicate balance of ecosystems. This deep-rooted connection makes women natural leaders in the fight against deforestation and the champions of reforestation efforts.

The act of planting a tree is a symbolic gesture of hope, a commitment to a brighter future. It is a tangible way to combat climate change, restore degraded lands, and protect biodiversity. Trees absorb carbon dioxide from the atmosphere, mitigate soil erosion, regulate water cycles, and provide habitat for wildlife. They also offer numerous social and economic benefits, such as improved air quality, increased agricultural productivity, and enhanced community well-being.

Women-led reforestation initiatives are springing up across the globe, demonstrating the power of collective action and the transformative potential of female leadership. These initiatives often combine tree planting with education, community empowerment, and sustainable livelihoods, creating a holistic approach to environmental restoration. They empower women with the knowledge and skills to manage forests sustainably, providing them with income-generating opportunities and a voice in decision-making processes.

In many parts of the world, women are disproportionately affected by deforestation and land degradation. They are often responsible for collecting firewood and water, tasks that become increasingly difficult as forests disappear. Reforestation efforts led by women not only address these immediate needs but also empower women to become agents of change in their communities, improving their livelihoods and strengthening their resilience in the face of environmental challenges.

The success of women-led reforestation initiatives is evident in various regions across the globe. In Africa, the Green Belt Movement, founded by Wangari Maathai, has empowered millions of women to plant trees, restore degraded lands, and advocate for environmental protection. In India, the Chipko movement, a grassroots women's movement, has successfully protected forests from commercial exploitation. And in Brazil, women are playing a leading role in the fight against deforestation in the Amazon rainforest.

These examples demonstrate the power of women to mobilize communities, inspire action, and create lasting change. They show that reforestation is not just about planting trees; it is about empowering women, building resilience, and fostering a sense of hope for the future.

"She Who Plants a Tree, Plants Hope" is a call to action for women everywhere to join the movement to reforest our planet. It is a guide to the principles and practices of reforestation, from selecting the right tree species to ensuring their long-term survival. It is also a celebration of the women who are leading the way in this vital endeavor, sharing their stories of success, challenges, and unwavering commitment.

The guide emphasizes the importance of community-based approaches to reforestation. It highlights the need to involve local women in every stage of the process, from planning and decision-making to implementation and monitoring. This not only ensures the success of reforestation efforts but also empowers women and strengthens their communities.

The guide also stresses the importance of using native tree species in reforestation projects. Native trees are adapted to the local climate and soil conditions, making them more likely to survive and thrive. They also play a vital role in maintaining the ecological balance of the region, providing habitat for native wildlife and supporting biodiversity.

Reforestation is not a quick fix for the environmental challenges we face. It is a long-term commitment that requires patience, perseverance, and collaboration. But the rewards are immeasurable. By planting trees, we are not only restoring the health of our planet, but we are also creating a more sustainable and equitable future for all.

So let us join hands with the women who are planting seeds of hope around the world. Let us embrace our role as stewards of the earth and work together to reforest our planet. Let us remember that every tree we plant is a gift to future generations, a symbol of our love for the earth, and a testament to the power of women to create a brighter tomorrow.

ᗕᗕᗕ

"Like the branches of a tree reaching for the sky, a woman's aspirations know no bounds. Let us rise together, creating a canopy of empowerment and change."

TEN

THE ART OF ARBORICULTURE: A WOMAN'S TOUCH IN TREE CULTIVATION.

In the intricate dance between humans and nature, the art of arboriculture emerges as a harmonious expression of our interconnectedness with the plant world. Traditionally, this field has been dominated by men, but a growing number of women are now making their mark, bringing a unique perspective and a nurturing touch to the cultivation of trees. "The Art of Arboriculture: A Woman's Touch in Tree Cultivation" delves into this evolving landscape, exploring the contributions of women arborists and the feminine energy they infuse into this age-old practice.

Arboriculture, the cultivation, management, and study of trees, is a multifaceted discipline that requires both scientific knowledge and an intuitive understanding of nature's rhythms. Women, with their innate connection to the earth and their nurturing instincts, are naturally drawn to this field, where they can apply their skills and passion to cultivate and care for these majestic living beings.

The history of arboriculture is replete with examples of women who have made significant contributions to the field. From pioneering botanists like Jane Colden, who documented the flora of New York in the 18th century, to modern-day arborists like Sharon Lilly, who has dedicated her career to tree care and education, women have played a vital role in advancing our understanding of trees and their importance in our lives.

Women arborists bring a unique perspective to the field, often emphasizing the importance of holistic approaches to tree care. They recognize that trees are not isolated entities but rather integral parts of complex ecosystems. They advocate for practices that promote biodiversity, soil health, and water conservation, recognizing that the well-being of trees is inextricably linked to the health of the environment as a whole.

One of the most distinctive qualities that women bring to arboriculture is their nurturing touch. Women are often drawn to the caregiving aspects of the profession, such as planting, pruning, and maintaining trees. They have a keen eye for detail and a deep understanding of the needs of individual trees, ensuring that each one receives the care and attention it requires to thrive.

Women arborists also excel at building relationships with trees. They understand that trees are not just objects to be managed but rather living beings with their own unique personalities and needs. By establishing a rapport with trees, women arborists are able to anticipate their needs and provide them with the optimal care.

The feminine approach to arboriculture is not limited to the technical aspects of tree care. Women are also playing a leading role in educating the public about the importance of trees and inspiring others to become involved in their preservation. They are writing books, giving talks, and leading workshops that teach people how to identify, plant, and care for trees. They are also active in advocacy efforts, working to protect forests from development and promoting sustainable forestry practices.

The contributions of women arborists are not only enriching the field of arboriculture but also transforming the way we think about our relationship with trees. Their holistic approach, nurturing touch, and passion for education are inspiring a new generation of tree lovers and environmental stewards.

The art of arboriculture is a dynamic and ever-evolving field, and women are at the forefront of this evolution. They are bringing fresh perspectives, innovative ideas, and a deep commitment to the well-being of trees and the planet. Their work is a testament to the power of women to create positive change and a reminder that we all have a role to play in protecting our natural heritage.

As we look to the future, it is clear that the role of women in arboriculture will only continue to grow. Their passion, expertise, and dedication are essential to the preservation of our forests and the cultivation of a more sustainable and harmonious relationship with the natural world. Let us celebrate the contributions of women arborists and support their efforts to create a greener and more beautiful planet for all.

ᏢᏢᏢ

"In the rustling leaves, we hear the whispers of our ancestors, the women who tended the land and passed down their wisdom. Let us honor their legacy by becoming stewards of the earth."

ELEVEN

Leave a Legacy in Leaves: A Practical Guide to Planting Trees.

In the grand tapestry of life, trees stand as timeless symbols of growth, resilience, and interconnectedness. They are the lungs of our planet, the guardians of our soil, and the providers of shade, shelter, and sustenance for countless creatures. Yet, in our modern world, we often overlook their importance, taking for granted the myriad benefits they offer. "

Leave a Legacy in Leaves" is a practical guide to planting trees, a call to action for individuals and communities to embrace the transformative power of these arboreal wonders and create a lasting legacy for generations to come.

The act of planting a tree is a simple yet profound gesture, a tangible expression of our hope for the future. It is an investment in the health of our planet, a gift to future generations, and a testament to our commitment to environmental stewardship.

But beyond the ecological benefits, planting trees is also a deeply personal and meaningful experience. It connects us to the natural world, fosters a sense of community, and allows us to leave a lasting legacy that will outlive us all.

The journey begins with understanding the significance of trees in our ecosystem. Trees are not merely ornamental additions to our landscapes; they are essential components of a complex web of life. They absorb carbon dioxide, a major greenhouse gas, and release oxygen, the lifeblood of our planet.

Their roots bind the soil, preventing erosion and filtering rainwater, while their branches provide habitat and sustenance for a myriad of creatures. By planting trees, we are not only beautifying our surroundings but also actively contributing to the health and resilience of our planet.

Choosing the right tree for the right place is the first step towards a successful planting. Consider your local climate, soil type, available space, and the purpose of your planting. Are you looking for shade, privacy, fruit, or ornamental beauty? Each tree species has unique characteristics and requirements, so it's essential to do your research and select trees that are well-suited to your specific environment.

Once you've chosen your trees, it's time to prepare the planting site. This involves clearing the area of weeds and debris, digging a hole twice as wide as the root ball and just as deep, and amending the soil with compost or other organic matter to improve drainage and fertility. Proper planting technique is crucial for the tree's survival and long-term health.

After planting, your tree will need ongoing care and attention. Regular watering, especially during the first few years, is essential to establish a strong root system.

Mulching around the base of the tree helps to retain moisture, suppress weeds, and regulate soil temperature. Pruning, when done correctly, can promote healthy growth and improve the tree's structure.

Trees are not immune to pests and diseases, so it's important to monitor them regularly and take action if necessary. Early detection and intervention can often prevent minor problems from becoming major ones. Consult with a local arborist or extension service for advice on identifying and treating tree ailments.

Beyond the practical aspects of planting and care, trees offer a wealth of intangible benefits. They enhance the beauty of our landscapes, provide shade and cooling, reduce noise pollution, and create a sense of tranquility and well-being. Trees also have a positive impact on property values, making them a wise investment for homeowners and communities.

Planting trees is not only an act of environmental responsibility but also a way to build community and connect with others. Community tree-planting events bring people together for a common purpose, fostering a sense of camaraderie and shared ownership of the environment. They also provide opportunities for education and learning, as participants gain knowledge about trees and their care.

The legacy we leave in leaves is not just about the trees themselves but also about the stories they tell. Every tree has a story, a history that unfolds over time.

It witnesses the changing seasons, the passing of years, and the lives of the people who live and work around it. By planting a tree, we are creating a living monument, a tangible reminder of our commitment to the future.

"Leave a Legacy in Leaves" is a guide for anyone who wants to make a difference in the world, one tree at a time. It is a practical resource for planting and caring for trees, but it is also an inspiration to embrace the transformative power of these arboreal wonders.

By planting trees, we are not only creating a greener and healthier planet, but we are also creating a legacy of hope, resilience, and interconnectedness that will endure for generations to come.

ᐅᐅᐅ

"A tree's embrace is a sanctuary for the soul. Seek solace in its shade, find strength in its roots, and let its wisdom guide you on your path."

TWELVE

A WOMAN'S GUIDE TO FORESTRY: EMPOWERING THE NEXT GENERATION OF TREE HUGGERS.

In the heart of the forest, where sunlight filters through the leaves and the air is alive with the sound of birdsong, lies a world of wonder and wisdom waiting to be discovered. Forestry, the science and art of managing forests, has traditionally been a male-dominated field. However, a growing number of women are now embracing this profession, bringing their unique perspectives, skills, and passion to the stewardship of our woodlands. "A Woman's Guide to Forestry: Empowering the Next Generation of Tree Huggers" is a celebration of this movement, a call to action for women and girls to explore the world of forestry and become champions for our planet's precious forests.

Forestry is a multifaceted discipline that encompasses a wide range of activities, from planting and caring for trees to managing wildlife habitats and protecting watersheds. It requires a deep understanding of ecology, botany, and silviculture, as well as a passion for the natural world. Women, with their innate connection to the earth and their nurturing instincts, are uniquely suited to excel in this field.

Historically, women have played a vital role in forest management, particularly in indigenous communities, where their knowledge of plants and ecosystems has been passed down through generations. However, in more recent times, women's contributions to forestry have often been overlooked or undervalued. This is changing, as more and more women are pursuing careers in forestry and taking on leadership roles in the field.

Women foresters bring a unique perspective to the profession, often emphasizing the importance of holistic and sustainable approaches to forest management. They recognize that forests are not simply collections of trees but complex ecosystems that provide a multitude of benefits to both humans and the environment. They advocate for practices that promote biodiversity, soil health, and water quality, while also recognizing the economic and social importance of forests.

One of the most inspiring aspects of women's involvement in forestry is their dedication to education and outreach. Many women foresters are passionate about sharing their knowledge and inspiring the next generation of tree huggers. They lead workshops, give talks, and mentor young women who are interested in pursuing careers in forestry. They also work to raise awareness about the importance of forests and the threats they face, such as deforestation, climate change, and invasive species.

The contributions of women foresters are not only enriching the field of forestry but also transforming the way we think about our relationship with forests. They are challenging traditional gender roles, breaking down barriers, and creating a more inclusive and equitable workplace. They are also demonstrating that forestry is not just a job but a calling, a way to connect with nature, make a difference in the world, and leave a lasting legacy for future generations.

"A Woman's Guide to Forestry" is an invitation for women and girls to explore the exciting world of forestry and discover the many career paths it offers. It provides practical advice on how to get started in the field, from choosing the right educational program to finding mentors and networking opportunities. It also highlights the diverse roles that women play in forestry, from research scientists to forest managers to educators and advocates.

The guide emphasizes the importance of mentorship and role models for young women who are interested in forestry. It showcases the stories of successful women foresters who have overcome challenges and achieved their goals. These stories serve as an inspiration and a reminder that with hard work, dedication, and passion, anything is possible.

The guide also addresses the unique challenges that women face in the forestry profession, such as gender bias, discrimination, and harassment. It provides resources and support for women who are navigating these challenges, empowering them to overcome obstacles and thrive in their careers.

Forestry is a field that is constantly evolving, and women are playing a leading role in shaping its future. They are bringing fresh perspectives, innovative ideas, and a deep commitment to sustainability and social justice. Their work is essential to the health of our planet and the well-being of future generations.

"A Woman's Guide to Forestry" is a celebration of the women who are leading the way in this vital field. It is a call to action for women and girls everywhere to embrace their passion for nature, pursue their dreams, and become the next generation of tree huggers. By working together, we can ensure that our forests are protected and managed sustainably for the benefit of all.

ᐅᐅᐅ

"The joy of growing is not just about nurturing trees; it is about nurturing our own spirits, finding purpose in the rhythm of the seasons, and cultivating a deeper connection to the natural world."

THIRTEEN

FROM SAPLING TO SUCCESS: A STEP-BY-STEP GUIDE TO TREE PLANTING.

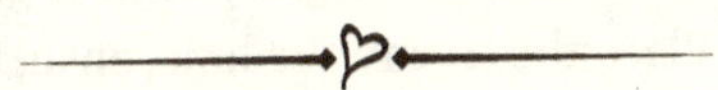

The journey of a tree, from a delicate sapling to a towering giant, is a testament to the resilience and wonder of nature. Each tree begins as a tiny seed, carrying within it the potential for growth, transformation, and a lasting legacy. "From Sapling to Success" is a practical guide that empowers individuals and communities to embark on this journey, providing step-by-step instructions and valuable insights to ensure the successful planting and nurturing of trees.

Step 1. Choosing the Right Tree

The foundation of successful tree planting lies in selecting the right tree for the right place. Consider your local climate, soil type, available space, and the purpose of your planting. Native trees are often the best choice, as they are well-adapted to the local conditions and require less maintenance. Research different species and their growth habits to determine which ones are best suited to your specific needs and preferences.

Step 2. Preparing the Planting Site

Once you have chosen your tree, it's time to prepare the planting site. Clear the area of grass, weeds, and debris. Dig a hole that is twice as wide as the tree's root ball and just as deep. This will allow the roots to spread out and establish themselves firmly in the soil. Loosen the soil at the bottom of the hole to improve drainage and aeration.

Step 3. Planting the Tree

Gently remove the tree from its container, being careful not to damage the roots. If the roots are tightly bound, gently loosen them with your fingers. Place the tree in the hole, ensuring that the top of the root ball is level with the surrounding ground. Backfill the hole with soil, tamping it down gently to eliminate air pockets.

Step 4. Watering and Mulching

Water the tree thoroughly after planting, soaking the entire root zone. Add a layer of mulch around the base of the tree, leaving a few inches of space around the trunk. Mulch helps to retain moisture, suppress weeds, and regulate soil temperature, creating a favorable environment for root growth.

Step 5. Staking and Protecting

If your tree is tall or planted in a windy area, it may need staking for support. Use two or three stakes placed evenly around the tree and loosely tie them to the trunk with soft material to avoid damage. Additionally, consider protecting your tree from pests and animals by using tree guards or repellents.

Step 6. Ongoing Care

The journey doesn't end with planting. Trees require ongoing care and attention to thrive. Water regularly, especially during dry periods, and fertilize according to the needs of your specific tree species. Prune dead or diseased branches to maintain the tree's health and shape. Monitor for pests and diseases, and take action if necessary.

Beyond the Basics

Successful tree planting involves more than just following the steps outlined above. It requires a deep understanding of tree biology, soil science, and environmental factors. It also involves a commitment to long-term stewardship, as trees can live for decades or even centuries.

Here are some additional tips for maximizing your tree-planting success:

Plant in the right season: Spring and fall are generally the best times to plant trees, as the weather is mild and conducive to root growth.

Choose healthy trees: Select trees that are free of pests and diseases, and have a well-developed root system.

Consider the mature size of the tree: Avoid planting trees too close to buildings, power lines, or other structures that could be damaged by their growth.

Water deeply and infrequently: A deep watering once a week is better than shallow watering every day.

Fertilize sparingly: Over-fertilizing can damage trees. Follow the recommendations for your specific tree species.

Prune regularly: Proper pruning promotes healthy growth and prevents structural problems.

Protect from pests and diseases: Monitor your trees regularly and take action if you notice any signs of trouble.

By following these steps and tips, you can ensure that your trees thrive and provide years of enjoyment and environmental benefits. Remember, planting a tree is an investment in the future, a gift to generations to come. It is a symbol of hope, resilience, and the enduring power of nature.

❧❧❧

"In the heart of every seed lies the promise of a new beginning. Let us sow the seeds of change and watch them blossom into a brighter future."

FOURTEEN

CULTIVATING CONNECTIONS: HOW TREES CAN HEAL AND TRANSFORM.

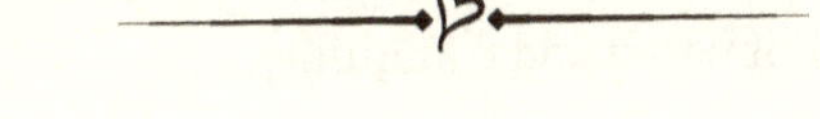

In the intricate tapestry of life, trees emerge as silent yet powerful healers, weaving their magic into the very fabric of our existence. Their presence extends far beyond their physical form, touching our hearts, minds, and souls in profound ways. "Cultivating Connections: How Trees Can Heal and Transform" delves into the intricate relationship between humans and trees, exploring the myriad ways in which these arboreal wonders can mend our spirits, restore our connection to nature, and inspire positive change.

The healing power of trees is deeply rooted in our evolutionary history. For millennia, humans have sought refuge, sustenance, and solace in the embrace of forests. Trees have provided us with shelter, food, medicine, and materials for tools and shelter. This deep-seated connection to trees is reflected in our cultural traditions, myths, and folklore, where trees are often revered as symbols of wisdom, strength, and longevity.

In recent times, scientific research has begun to unravel the physiological and psychological benefits of spending time in nature, particularly among trees. Studies have shown that exposure to trees can reduce stress, lower blood pressure, boost the immune system, and improve mood and cognitive function. The Japanese practice of "forest bathing," or shinrin-yoku, has gained popularity worldwide as a way to immerse oneself in the healing atmosphere of the forest.

The therapeutic effects of trees can be attributed to a variety of factors. Trees release phytoncides, airborne chemicals that have been shown to have antimicrobial and immune-boosting properties. The sight, sound, and smell of trees also have a calming effect on our nervous system, reducing stress hormones and promoting relaxation. The fractal patterns of leaves and branches can induce a meditative state, while the gentle swaying of trees in the breeze can lull us into a sense of peace and tranquility.

Beyond the physical and psychological benefits, trees also have a profound impact on our spiritual well-being. Many cultures believe that trees have souls or spirits, and that they can serve as conduits for communication with the divine. In some traditions, trees are seen as sacred guardians, protecting the land and its inhabitants. Spending time among trees can evoke a sense of awe and wonder, reminding us of our place in the grand scheme of things.

Trees also play a vital role in healing communities and fostering social connections. Community tree-planting projects bring people together from all walks of life, united by a common purpose. They provide opportunities for collaboration, learning, and shared experiences. Trees can also serve as gathering places, creating spaces for connection, conversation, and celebration.

The transformative power of trees is evident in their ability to inspire positive change. Trees have been planted to commemorate significant events, honor loved ones, and mark milestones in our lives. They have been used to restore degraded lands, create urban green spaces, and mitigate the effects of climate change. Trees are symbols of hope, resilience, and the enduring power of nature to heal and renew.

In a world that is increasingly disconnected from nature, trees offer a vital link to the natural world. They remind us of our dependence on the earth and the importance of living in harmony with our environment. They teach us valuable lessons about patience, resilience, and the interconnectedness of all living things.

Cultivating connections with trees is a journey of self-discovery and personal growth. It involves opening our hearts and minds to the wisdom of the natural world, and allowing ourselves to be transformed by its beauty and power. It is a process of slowing down, tuning in to our senses, and appreciating the simple joys of being in nature.

Whether you are planting a tree in your backyard, volunteering at a local park, or simply taking a walk in the woods, you are participating in a powerful act of healing and transformation. By cultivating connections with trees, you are not only improving your own well-being but also contributing to the health of our planet and the future of our children.

So let us all embrace the healing power of trees. Let us plant them, nurture them, and learn from them. Let us create a world where trees are valued and protected, where forests flourish, and where people and nature thrive together.

ᐅᐅᐅ

"The symphony of green is a song of hope, a melody of resilience, and a chorus of interconnectedness. Let us join our voices with the trees and sing a new song of healing for our planet."

FIFTEEN

TREES AS TEACHERS: LESSONS IN SUSTAINABILITY FROM NATURE.

In the quiet grandeur of a forest, amidst the rustling leaves and dappled sunlight, lies a profound wisdom waiting to be unveiled. Trees, the silent sentinels of the Earth, have much to teach us about sustainability, resilience, and the interconnectedness of all living things. "Trees as Teachers" is an exploration of these invaluable lessons, drawing inspiration from nature's wisdom to guide us towards a more harmonious and sustainable way of life.

Trees, in their silent wisdom, embody the very essence of sustainability. They thrive in a delicate balance with their environment, taking only what they need and giving back in abundance. Their leaves absorb carbon dioxide, a major greenhouse gas, and release oxygen, the lifeblood of our planet.

Their roots anchor the soil, preventing erosion and filtering rainwater, while their branches provide habitat and sustenance for a myriad of creatures.

One of the most fundamental lessons trees teach us is the importance of interconnectedness. Trees are not isolated entities; they are integral parts of complex ecosystems, where every organism, from the tiniest microbe to the largest mammal, plays a crucial role.

The health of the forest depends on the well-being of all its inhabitants, and any disruption to this delicate balance can have far-reaching consequences.

Trees also exemplify the concept of resilience. They have evolved to withstand a wide range of environmental conditions, from droughts and floods to pests and diseases. When faced with adversity, trees adapt and find ways to survive, often emerging stronger and more resilient than before. This resilience is a valuable lesson for humans, who are also facing unprecedented environmental challenges.

Another important lesson trees teach us is the value of long-term thinking. Trees are not concerned with immediate gratification; they invest in their future by growing slowly and steadily, year after year. They patiently build their roots, strengthen their trunks, and extend their branches, ensuring their survival for generations to come.

This long-term perspective is essential for sustainability, as it encourages us to consider the impact of our actions on future generations and to make choices that benefit both present and future needs.

Trees also demonstrate the importance of diversity. A healthy forest is a diverse forest, with a wide variety of tree species, ages, and sizes. This diversity creates a resilient ecosystem that is better able to withstand disturbances and adapt to changing conditions. Similarly, human societies thrive on diversity, where different perspectives, experiences, and skills contribute to a richer and more vibrant community.

The lessons trees teach us about sustainability extend beyond the ecological realm. Trees also have a profound impact on our physical and mental health. Studies have shown that spending time in nature, particularly among trees, can reduce stress, lower blood pressure, boost the immune system, and improve mood and cognitive function.

Trees provide a sense of tranquility and connection to the natural world, offering a refuge from the hustle and bustle of modern life.

The practice of forest bathing, or shinrin-yoku, is a Japanese tradition that involves immersing oneself in the forest atmosphere to promote health and well-being. This practice has gained popularity worldwide as people seek to reconnect with nature and experience the therapeutic benefits of trees.

Trees also play a vital role in our cultural and spiritual traditions. Many cultures revere trees as sacred symbols, associating them with wisdom, strength, and longevity. Trees have inspired countless works of art, literature, and music, and they continue to serve as a source of inspiration for people around the world.

In a world facing unprecedented environmental challenges, the wisdom of trees offers a beacon of hope. By learning from their example, we can cultivate a more sustainable way of life that respects the interconnectedness of all living things, values long-term thinking, and embraces diversity.

We can create communities that are resilient, adaptable, and thriving, just like the forests that sustain us.

"Trees as Teachers" is an invitation to reconnect with nature, to listen to the wisdom of trees, and to apply their teachings to our own lives.

It is a call to action to protect and restore our forests, to plant trees in our communities, and to embrace a more sustainable way of life. By honoring the wisdom of trees, we can create a brighter future for ourselves, our children, and the planet we call home.

ᗺᗺᗺ

*"From sapling to success, the journey of a tree is a
lesson in perseverance and growth. Let us embrace
this journey, nurturing our dreams and aspirations
like the tender shoots of a young tree."*

SIXTEEN

THE GREEN GODDESS GUIDE: UNLEASHING YOUR INNER ARBORIST.

Deep within each of us lies an innate connection to the natural world, a primal instinct that draws us to the verdant embrace of trees. "The Green Goddess Guide" is an invitation to awaken this inner arborist, to tap into the wisdom of the trees, and to cultivate a harmonious relationship with these majestic beings.

This guide is not just about planting and caring for trees; it is about embracing a lifestyle that celebrates the interconnectedness of all living things, a lifestyle that nurtures both the environment and our souls.

The Green Goddess is an archetype that embodies the feminine energy of nature, the nurturing spirit that sustains and nourishes all life on Earth. She is the embodiment of the forest, the guardian of the trees, and the source of their wisdom.

By connecting with the Green Goddess within ourselves, we can tap into our own innate wisdom and discover our unique role in the web of life.

Trees, as the Green Goddess's most beloved creations, hold a special significance in this journey. They are not merely objects to be admired or exploited; they are sentient beings with their own unique personalities, wisdom, and healing powers.

By learning to communicate with trees, we can unlock a wealth of knowledge about the natural world and gain valuable insights into our own lives.

The first step on this journey is to cultivate a sense of reverence for trees. Take the time to observe them in their natural habitat, noticing their unique shapes, textures, and colors. Listen to the rustling of their leaves, feel the roughness of their bark, and inhale the fragrance of their blossoms. Allow yourself to be fully present in the moment, immersing yourself in the sights, sounds, and smells of the forest.

As you deepen your connection with trees, you may begin to notice subtle shifts in your own energy and awareness. You may feel a sense of calm and tranquility, a feeling of being grounded and centered.

You may also begin to experience a heightened sense of intuition and creativity. These are all signs that you are tapping into the wisdom of the trees and awakening your inner arborist.

The Green Goddess Guide encourages you to explore various practices that can deepen your connection with trees. These practices include:

Tree Hugging: A simple yet powerful way to connect with a tree's energy. Embrace the trunk of the tree with your arms and press your cheek against its bark. Close your eyes and breathe deeply, allowing yourself to feel the tree's energy flowing into your body.

Tree Meditation: Find a quiet spot in the forest and sit with your back against a tree. Close your eyes and focus on your breath, allowing your mind to quiet down. As you relax, you may begin to feel a sense of connection with the tree, as if you are merging with its energy.

Tree Communication: Trees communicate through subtle vibrations and energy fields. To communicate with a tree, simply approach it with an open heart and mind. Speak to it silently or aloud, sharing your thoughts, feelings, and intentions. You may be surprised at the insights and wisdom that the tree shares with you in return.

Tree Planting and Care: Planting and caring for trees is a tangible way to express your love and gratitude for these magnificent beings. By nurturing trees, you are also nurturing the Green Goddess within yourself and contributing to the health of the planet.

As you embark on this journey of self-discovery and environmental stewardship, remember that the Green Goddess is always with you, guiding and supporting you every step of the way.

She is the embodiment of nature's wisdom, the source of our strength and resilience. By connecting with her, we can tap into our own inner power and become agents of positive change in the world.

The Green Goddess Guide is more than just a set of instructions; it is a philosophy of life, a way of being in the world that honors the interconnectedness of all living things. It is a call to embrace our role as stewards of the Earth, to protect and nurture the natural world, and to create a more harmonious and sustainable future for all.

So let us awaken our inner arborists, let us connect with the Green Goddess within ourselves, and let us cultivate a deeper relationship with the trees that sustain us. By doing so, we not only honor the Earth but also nourish our own souls and contribute to a brighter future for all.

ᗡᗡᗡ

"In the forest, we find our true selves, stripped of the masks we wear in the outside world. Let us shed our burdens and embrace the healing embrace of nature."

SEVENTEEN

PLANTING SEEDS OF EMPOWERMENT: WOMEN LEADING THE WAY IN CONSERVATION.

In the intricate dance between humanity and the environment, women have long held a unique and vital role. Their innate connection to the earth, nurturing instincts, and traditional ecological knowledge have positioned them as powerful agents of change in the realm of conservation. "Planting Seeds of Empowerment" explores this dynamic, illuminating how women are leading the way in environmental stewardship, fostering sustainable practices, and inspiring a new generation of conservationists.

Throughout history, women have been the custodians of nature's bounty, their lives intertwined with the rhythms of the earth. They have been the gatherers of wild foods, the cultivators of crops, and the healers who harness the power of plants for medicine. Their intimate knowledge of local ecosystems, passed down through generations, has been essential for the survival and well-being of their communities.

In recent decades, women's leadership in conservation has gained significant momentum, challenging traditional gender roles and redefining the narrative of environmentalism. Women are not only passionate advocates for nature but also skilled scientists, researchers, policymakers, and community organizers. They bring a unique perspective to conservation, often emphasizing the interconnectedness of social, economic, and environmental issues.

One of the most striking examples of women's leadership in conservation is the Green Belt Movement, founded by the late Wangari Maathai, a Kenyan environmentalist and Nobel Peace Prize laureate. Maathai recognized the devastating impact of deforestation on women's livelihoods and the environment, and she mobilized rural women to plant trees, restore degraded lands, and advocate for sustainable practices. The Green Belt Movement not only transformed the landscape of Kenya but also empowered women economically and politically, demonstrating the transformative power of grassroots action.

Women are also at the forefront of efforts to protect biodiversity and combat climate change. They are leading research on the impacts of climate change on vulnerable communities, developing innovative solutions for sustainable agriculture, and advocating for policies that reduce greenhouse gas emissions. Their expertise and leadership are crucial for addressing the complex and interconnected challenges facing our planet.

The empowerment of women in conservation is not only a matter of justice and equality; it is also a strategic imperative. Studies have shown that when women are empowered, they invest more in their families and communities, leading to improved health, education, and economic outcomes. This, in turn, contributes to greater environmental sustainability, as empowered women are more likely to adopt environmentally friendly practices and advocate for policies that protect the planet.

Women's leadership in conservation is not limited to formal organizations and institutions. It is also evident in the countless grassroots initiatives led by women around the world. These initiatives often focus on local issues, such as water conservation, waste management, and sustainable agriculture. By empowering women at the grassroots level, we can create a ripple effect of positive change that extends far beyond the immediate community.

The rise of women in conservation is not without its challenges. Women often face discrimination, lack of access to resources, and cultural barriers that hinder their participation in decision-making processes. However, these challenges have not deterred women from pursuing their passion for the environment. On the contrary, they have fueled their determination to create a more inclusive and equitable space for women in conservation.

One of the most inspiring aspects of women's leadership in conservation is their ability to build bridges and foster collaboration. They recognize that environmental issues cannot be solved in isolation and that we need to work together across sectors and disciplines to find sustainable solutions. Women are often skilled at building relationships, facilitating dialogue, and finding common ground, making them effective leaders in collaborative conservation efforts.

The stories of women leading the way in conservation are a testament to the power of passion, perseverance, and collective action. They inspire us to believe that a better future is possible, one where humans and nature can thrive together. They remind us that each of us has a role to play in protecting our planet, no matter how small or insignificant it may seem.

"Planting Seeds of Empowerment" is a celebration of the women who are leading the way in conservation. It is a call to action for all of us to support their efforts, to amplify their voices, and to create a world where women's leadership in environmental stewardship is not only valued but also celebrated. By working together, we can plant the seeds of a more sustainable and equitable future, a future where all living beings can flourish.

🌱🌱🌱

"Like the roots of a tree that bind the soil together,
women are the glue that holds communities
together. Let us strengthen these bonds and build a
more resilient and equitable world."

EIGHTEEN

THE JOY OF GROWING: A CELEBRATION OF TREES AND THE WOMEN WHO LOVE THEM.

In the intricate dance of life, there exists a profound connection between women and trees, a bond forged through shared experiences of nurturing, growth, and resilience. "The Joy of Growing" is a celebration of this beautiful relationship, exploring the myriad ways in which trees enrich our lives and the unique perspectives women bring to their care and appreciation.

The deep-rooted affinity between women and trees is woven into the fabric of human history and culture. In ancient mythologies, goddesses were often associated with trees, symbolizing fertility, wisdom, and the cyclical nature of life.

Women have long been the gatherers of fruits and nuts, the weavers of baskets and textiles from bark and leaves, and the healers who harness the medicinal properties of plants. Their intimate knowledge of the natural world, passed down through generations, has been essential for the survival and well-being of their communities.

In modern times, this connection between women and trees continues to flourish, manifesting in diverse forms of expression. Women are passionate gardeners, nurturing seedlings into thriving plants and cultivating vibrant landscapes. They are avid hikers and nature enthusiasts, finding solace and inspiration in the embrace of forests.

They are scientists and researchers, unlocking the secrets of tree biology and advocating for their conservation. And they are artists, writers, and musicians, drawing inspiration from the beauty and majesty of trees to create works that touch our hearts and souls.

The joy of growing is not merely about the physical act of planting and nurturing trees; it is about the emotional, spiritual, and intellectual nourishment that trees provide. They offer us a sense of connection to the natural world, a reminder of our place in the grand scheme of things. They teach us about resilience, adaptability, and the importance of community. They inspire us with their beauty, grace, and unwavering strength.

Women, with their innate nurturing instincts, bring a unique perspective to the appreciation and care of trees. They understand the importance of patience, observation, and gentle guidance in cultivating growth. They recognize that trees, like humans, have individual personalities and needs, and they respond with empathy and compassion. They celebrate the diversity of tree species, appreciating the unique beauty and value of each one.

The joy of growing is also about sharing our passion for trees with others. Women have been instrumental in educating communities about the importance of trees and inspiring others to become involved in their care.

They have led tree-planting initiatives, organized educational workshops, and advocated for policies that protect forests. Their enthusiasm and dedication have sparked a growing movement of tree lovers and environmental stewards.

The benefits of connecting with trees are manifold. Studies have shown that spending time in nature, particularly among trees, can reduce stress, lower blood pressure, boost the immune system, and improve mood and cognitive function. Trees also provide numerous environmental benefits, such as cleaning the air, filtering water, preventing soil erosion, and providing habitat for wildlife.

By planting and caring for trees, women are not only enhancing their own well-being but also contributing to the health of the planet.

The joy of growing is a celebration of life, a recognition of the interconnectedness of all living beings. It is a reminder that we are not separate from nature but rather an integral part of it. By nurturing trees, we are nurturing ourselves, our communities, and the planet we call home.

As we face the challenges of climate change and environmental degradation, the joy of growing takes on a new urgency.

Trees are essential for mitigating the impacts of climate change, absorbing carbon dioxide from the atmosphere, and providing a natural buffer against extreme weather events. Women, with their deep understanding of the natural world and their passion for its protection, are leading the way in reforestation and conservation efforts.

The joy of growing is a testament to the power of women to create positive change. It is a celebration of the women who have dedicated their lives to the care and preservation of trees, and it is an invitation for all women to embrace their role as stewards of the earth. By planting seeds of hope and nurturing the growth of trees, we can create a more beautiful, sustainable, and resilient future for generations to come.

ᗕᗕᗕ

"The legacy we leave in leaves is a testament to our love for the earth. Let us plant trees that will shade our children, clean our air, and inspire future generations."

NINETEEN

A Woman's Roots Run Deep: Finding Strength and Resilience Through Nature.

In the intricate tapestry of life, women have always held a profound connection with nature. Just as the roots of a tree anchor it to the earth, providing stability and nourishment, a woman's roots run deep into the natural world, drawing strength, resilience, and wisdom from its embrace. This essay explores the symbiotic relationship between women and nature, highlighting how the natural world can serve as a source of empowerment, healing, and personal growth.

The roots of this connection can be traced back to our earliest ancestors, who lived in close harmony with the environment. Women were the gatherers of wild foods, the cultivators of crops, and the caretakers of the land. They understood the rhythms of nature, the cycles of life and death, and the delicate balance of ecosystems. This intimate knowledge of the natural world fostered a deep respect for its power and a sense of responsibility for its well-being.

In many cultures, women have been associated with the earth, representing fertility, abundance, and the creative force of life. They have been revered as goddesses of nature, embodying the power of the elements and the cycles of the seasons. This connection to the feminine principle of nature has imbued women with a deep understanding of the interconnectedness of all living things, a sense of belonging to the natural world, and a reverence for its wisdom.

In modern times, as our lives have become increasingly urbanized and disconnected from nature, the importance of this connection has become even more apparent. Studies have shown that spending time in nature can reduce stress, improve mood, boost creativity, and enhance overall well-being. For women, who often juggle multiple roles and responsibilities, the natural world can offer a much-needed respite from the demands of daily life.

Nature provides a space for reflection, introspection, and rejuvenation. The quiet solitude of a forest, the gentle lapping of waves on a shoreline, or the awe-inspiring sight of a mountain peak can all awaken a sense of wonder and appreciation for the beauty and power of the natural world. This connection to nature can help women tap into their inner strength and resilience, providing them with the resources they need to face challenges and overcome adversity.

The natural world also offers valuable lessons in resilience and adaptability. Trees that bend in the wind but do not break, flowers that bloom in the harshest conditions, and animals that migrate thousands of miles in search of food and shelter all demonstrate the power of adaptation and the will to survive. By observing these examples in nature, women can learn to navigate life's challenges with grace and determination.

Nature also provides a sense of perspective. In the grand scheme of things, our individual problems may seem small and insignificant. The vastness of the ocean, the age-old mountains, and the endless expanse of the sky remind us of our place in the universe and the fleeting nature of our own existence. This perspective can help women to let go of worries and anxieties, to focus on what truly matters, and to live more fully in the present moment.

For many women, nature is a source of creative inspiration. The colors, textures, and patterns of the natural world have inspired countless works of art, literature, and music. Spending time in nature can spark creativity, ignite imagination, and open up new possibilities. It can also provide a sense of calm and focus that is conducive to creative expression.

The connection between women and nature is not only a source of personal strength and resilience but also a catalyst for social change. Women have been at the forefront of environmental movements, advocating for the protection of forests, oceans, and wildlife. They have organized grassroots campaigns, lobbied for policy changes, and raised awareness about environmental issues. Their passion and commitment have made a significant impact on the way we view and interact with the natural world.

A woman's roots run deep into the natural world, drawing strength, resilience, and wisdom from its embrace. By cultivating this connection, women can tap into their inner power, find solace and inspiration, and become agents of positive change in the world. Whether it's through spending time in nature, advocating for environmental protection, or simply appreciating the beauty of the natural world, women can find strength and resilience in their roots. So let us all embrace the power of nature, let us deepen our connection to the earth, and let us celebrate the unique bond between women and the natural world.

ᑭᑭᑭ

"A woman's intuition is a powerful tool for understanding the needs of the natural world. Let us trust our instincts and become advocates for the planet."

TWENTY

GROWING TOGETHER: BUILDING COMMUNITY THROUGH TREES.

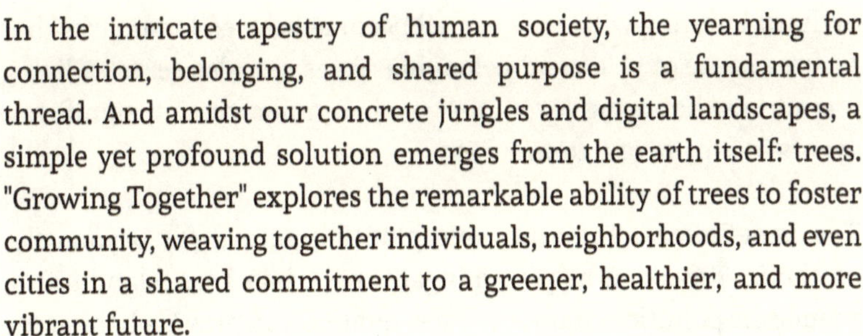

In the intricate tapestry of human society, the yearning for connection, belonging, and shared purpose is a fundamental thread. And amidst our concrete jungles and digital landscapes, a simple yet profound solution emerges from the earth itself: trees. "Growing Together" explores the remarkable ability of trees to foster community, weaving together individuals, neighborhoods, and even cities in a shared commitment to a greener, healthier, and more vibrant future.

Trees are not merely passive elements in our environment; they are living organisms that breathe, grow, and interact with their surroundings. They provide shade, clean air, and habitat for wildlife, creating a sense of place and a connection to the natural world. But beyond their ecological benefits, trees possess a unique power to bring people together, fostering a sense of community and shared purpose.

The act of planting a tree is a symbolic gesture of hope, a commitment to the future, and a tangible way to make a difference in our world. It is an act of collaboration, as individuals come together to dig, plant, and nurture a new life. This shared experience creates a bond between people, fostering a sense of camaraderie and shared ownership of the environment.

Community tree planting projects have become increasingly popular in recent years, as people recognize the power of trees to transform neighborhoods and improve quality of life. These projects bring together people from diverse backgrounds, ages, and walks of life, united by a common goal. They create opportunities for interaction, dialogue, and collaboration, breaking down barriers and building bridges between neighbors.

Trees also provide a sense of place and identity, anchoring communities to their surroundings. A majestic oak tree in a park, a row of flowering cherry trees lining a street, or a community orchard bursting with fruit can all become beloved landmarks that foster a sense of pride and belonging. Trees can also serve as living memorials, honoring loved ones and commemorating significant events in the life of a community.

The benefits of community tree planting extend far beyond the aesthetic. Trees can help to mitigate the urban heat island effect, reduce air pollution, improve water quality, and provide habitat for wildlife. They can also create a sense of safety and security, as well as opportunities for recreation and physical activity.

In neighborhoods where trees are abundant, residents report feeling more connected to their community, more satisfied with their surroundings, and more likely to engage in civic activities. Trees create a sense of shared ownership and responsibility, encouraging people to take pride in their neighborhoods and to work together to maintain and improve them.

The power of trees to build community is not limited to urban areas. In rural communities, trees play a vital role in supporting livelihoods, providing food, fuel, and building materials. Community forestry projects can empower local communities to manage their forests sustainably, ensuring that they continue to provide these essential resources for generations to come.

Trees also have a unique ability to heal and restore communities that have been affected by trauma or disaster. In the aftermath of Hurricane Katrina, for example, community tree planting projects played a crucial role in helping residents to rebuild their lives and their neighborhoods. Trees provided shade, beauty, and a sense of hope in the midst of devastation.

The connection between trees and community is not a new one. Throughout history, trees have served as gathering places, sites of worship, and symbols of cultural identity. The ancient Greeks held their assemblies under sacred oak trees, while Native American tribes gathered around council fires beneath the branches of giant sequoias. Trees have witnessed births, deaths, marriages, and other significant events in the lives of countless communities.

In our modern world, where technology often isolates us from one another, trees offer a way to reconnect with our neighbors and our communities. They provide a reason to come together, to work towards a common goal, and to celebrate the beauty and bounty of nature. By planting and caring for trees together, we are not only creating a greener and healthier environment but also strengthening the bonds that unite us as a community.

"Growing Together" is a celebration of the power of trees to build community, to heal wounds, and to foster hope. It is a call to action for individuals and communities to embrace the transformative power of trees and to work together to create a more sustainable, equitable, and vibrant future for all.

ppp

"The art of arboriculture is a dance between science
and intuition, a harmonious blend of knowledge
and love. Let us embrace this art and cultivate a
deeper connection to the trees."

TWENTY-ONE

THE CANOPY OF CHANGE: HOW TREES CAN REVITALIZE OUR PLANET.

In the intricate ballet of nature, trees stand as graceful dancers, their branches swaying in the breeze, their leaves whispering secrets to the wind. Yet, beneath their serene facade lies a profound power, a capacity to heal, to restore, and to revitalize our planet. "The Canopy of Change" explores this transformative power, illuminating how trees, in their quiet majesty, hold the key to a more sustainable and vibrant future.

Trees are not merely passive bystanders in the drama of life; they are active participants, playing a vital role in maintaining the delicate balance of our ecosystem. They are the lungs of our planet, inhaling carbon dioxide, a major greenhouse gas, and exhaling oxygen, the lifeblood of all living beings. Their roots delve deep into the earth, anchoring the soil, preventing erosion, and filtering rainwater, ensuring the purity of our water sources. Their branches provide shelter and sustenance for a myriad of creatures, from birds and insects to mammals and reptiles, creating a vibrant tapestry of biodiversity.

The canopy of change begins with a single seed, a tiny vessel of hope that holds within it the promise of a new life. As the seed germinates and sends its roots into the earth, it embarks on a journey of growth and transformation. With each passing season, the tree grows taller, its branches reaching towards the sky, its leaves unfurling to capture the sun's energy. This growth is not only a testament to the resilience of nature but also a symbol of hope and renewal.

As trees mature, their canopies expand, creating a protective umbrella that shields the earth from the harsh rays of the sun. This shade not only provides relief from the heat but also helps to regulate the temperature of the planet, mitigating the effects of climate change. Trees also act as natural air purifiers, absorbing pollutants and releasing clean oxygen into the atmosphere. This is particularly important in urban areas, where air pollution can have a significant impact on human health.

The roots of trees play a crucial role in maintaining soil health and preventing erosion. They bind the soil together, preventing it from being washed away by rain and wind. They also help to aerate the soil, allowing water and nutrients to penetrate deep into the ground, nourishing other plants and microorganisms. In this way, trees create a fertile environment that supports a diverse range of life.

Trees also play a vital role in the water cycle. Their leaves intercept rainfall, slowing its descent to the ground and reducing the risk of flooding. Their roots absorb water from the soil, filtering it and releasing it back into the atmosphere through transpiration. This process helps to regulate the flow of water in rivers and streams, ensuring a steady supply for both humans and wildlife.

The benefits of trees extend beyond their ecological functions. They also have a profound impact on human health and well-being. Studies have shown that spending time in nature, particularly among trees, can reduce stress, lower blood pressure, boost the immune system, and improve mood and cognitive function. Trees provide a sense of tranquility and connection to the natural world, offering a refuge from the hustle and bustle of modern life.

The canopy of change is not just about individual trees; it is about the collective power of forests. Forests are complex ecosystems that provide a multitude of benefits, from regulating climate and protecting watersheds to supporting biodiversity and providing livelihoods for millions of people. When we lose forests, we lose not only trees but also the intricate web of life that they support.

The good news is that we have the power to reverse the trend of deforestation and restore the canopy of change. Through reforestation efforts, we can plant new trees, restore degraded lands, and create a more sustainable future for ourselves and for generations to come. This is not just an environmental imperative but also a moral one, as we have a responsibility to protect the planet and its inhabitants.

Reforestation is not a quick fix, but it is a powerful tool for mitigating climate change and restoring the health of our planet. By planting trees, we are investing in the future, creating a legacy that will benefit countless generations. We are also demonstrating our commitment to a more sustainable and equitable world, where humans and nature can thrive together.

The canopy of change is a symbol of hope, a reminder that even in the face of environmental challenges, we have the power to create a better future. Let us embrace this power, let us plant trees, and let us work together to restore the balance of nature. For in the words of the poet, "Someone's sitting in the shade today because someone planted a tree a long time ago." Let us be the ones who plant the seeds of change for a brighter tomorrow.

ᐅᐅᐅ

"In every seed, there is a spark of hope, a potential
for transformation, and a promise of a greener
tomorrow. Let us nurture these seeds and watch
them blossom."

TWENTY-TWO

A Woman's Touch: Nurturing Nature for a Sustainable Future.

Throughout history, women have shared a unique and intimate bond with the natural world, a relationship often characterized by nurturing, intuition, and a deep understanding of the interconnectedness of all living things. "A Woman's Touch" delves into this profound connection, exploring how women's unique perspectives, skills, and experiences are shaping a more sustainable future for our planet.

Historically, women have been the primary caretakers of the land, responsible for gathering food, cultivating crops, and managing natural resources. This intimate connection with the earth has fostered a deep understanding of ecological systems and the importance of sustainable practices. Women have traditionally held a wealth of knowledge about plants, animals, and the environment, passed down through generations of oral tradition and hands-on experience.

In many indigenous cultures, women are revered as guardians of the earth, embodying the feminine principle of creation and nurturing. They are often the keepers of traditional ecological knowledge, possessing a deep understanding of the delicate balance between humans and nature. This knowledge is not just theoretical; it is embodied in their daily practices, from seed saving and sustainable agriculture to herbal medicine and water conservation.

In modern times, as the world grapples with environmental challenges such as climate change, deforestation, and pollution, women's voices and leadership in conservation have become increasingly important. Women are not only passionate advocates for the environment but also scientists, researchers, policymakers, and community organizers who are driving innovative solutions and inspiring action.

One of the most striking aspects of women's leadership in conservation is their emphasis on a holistic approach that recognizes the interconnectedness of social, economic, and environmental issues. They understand that environmental degradation disproportionately affects women, who often bear the brunt of resource scarcity, food insecurity, and climate-related disasters. Therefore, their solutions tend to be more inclusive and equitable, addressing the root causes of environmental problems and empowering women to become agents of change.

Women-led conservation initiatives are flourishing around the world, demonstrating the power of feminine energy to create positive change. From grassroots movements to global organizations, women are leading the way in protecting forests, restoring degraded lands, and promoting sustainable practices.

They are educating their communities, empowering women and girls, and advocating for policies that protect the environment.

For example, the Green Belt Movement, founded by Kenyan environmentalist Wangari Maathai, has empowered millions of women to plant trees, restore degraded lands, and improve their livelihoods. The Chipko movement in India, a grassroots women's movement, has successfully protected forests from commercial exploitation. And in the Amazon rainforest, indigenous women are leading the fight against deforestation, protecting their ancestral lands and traditional way of life.

These examples demonstrate the power of women's leadership in conservation, their ability to mobilize communities, inspire action, and create lasting change. They also highlight the importance of recognizing and valuing women's traditional ecological knowledge, which is often overlooked or dismissed in mainstream conservation efforts.

Women's leadership in conservation is not limited to grassroots movements. Women are also increasingly taking on leadership roles in government agencies, international organizations, and academic institutions. They are bringing their unique perspectives, skills, and experiences to bear on complex environmental issues, challenging traditional paradigms, and advocating for more inclusive and equitable solutions.

The "woman's touch" in conservation is not just about the work that women do but also about the way they do it. Women often bring a collaborative and nurturing approach to their work, fostering partnerships, building trust, and empowering others to take action. They are skilled communicators, educators, and motivators, inspiring others to care for the environment and work towards a sustainable future.

The journey towards a more sustainable future is a long and challenging one, but women's contributions are essential for its success. By empowering women, we are not only promoting gender equality but also unlocking the full potential of humanity to address the environmental challenges we face.

"A Woman's Touch" is a celebration of the women who are nurturing nature and inspiring a new generation of environmental stewards. It is a reminder that we are all connected to the earth and that our actions have a profound impact on the planet's health. By embracing the feminine values of nurturing, collaboration, and interconnectedness, we can create a more sustainable and equitable future for all.

ᗡᗡᗡ

"The canopy of change is a living testament to the power of women to create a more sustainable and equitable world. Let us raise our voices and demand a seat at the table."

TWENTY-THREE

A Symphony of Green: Creating Harmony Through Tree Planting.

In the heart of nature's orchestra, trees stand as majestic players, their rustling leaves creating a symphony of green that resonates with the very soul of our planet. "A Symphony of Green" explores the profound impact of tree planting, not just as an environmental act but as a harmonious endeavor that weaves together ecological balance, community engagement, and personal well-being.

Imagine a world where every rustling leaf is a note, every swaying branch a melody, and every towering trunk a resonating chord. This is the symphony of green, a harmonious composition that speaks to the interconnectedness of all living beings.

Trees, as the primary players in this orchestra, orchestrate a symphony of life, their roots anchoring the soil, their branches reaching towards the sky, and their leaves filtering the air we breathe.

The symphony begins with a single note, a tiny seed planted in the earth. As the seed germinates and sends its roots down into the soil, it begins to connect with the intricate web of life that surrounds it. It draws nourishment from the earth, water from the rain, and energy from the sun.

As it grows, it becomes a part of a larger community, interacting with other plants, animals, and microorganisms, each playing its own unique role in the symphony.

The trees' leaves, like the strings of a violin, capture the sun's energy and transform it into food through photosynthesis. This process not only nourishes the tree but also releases oxygen into the atmosphere, sustaining life on our planet. The leaves also act as filters, absorbing pollutants and releasing clean air, creating a healthier environment for all living beings.

The branches of the trees, like the woodwinds of an orchestra, create a framework for life. They provide shelter for birds and other animals, creating a vibrant ecosystem where countless species thrive. They also offer shade and protection from the elements, making our cities and towns more livable.

The roots of the trees, like the percussion section of a symphony, anchor the soil and prevent erosion. They also play a crucial role in the water cycle, absorbing water from the ground and releasing it back into the atmosphere through transpiration. This process helps to regulate the climate, cool the air, and ensure a steady supply of fresh water.

As the trees mature, their individual notes blend together, creating a harmonious symphony of green. This symphony is not only pleasing to the ears but also essential for the health of our planet. Trees help to mitigate climate change by absorbing carbon dioxide from the atmosphere.

They protect watersheds, ensuring a clean and abundant supply of water. They provide habitat for wildlife, promoting biodiversity and ecological balance.

The symphony of green is not just about the trees themselves; it is also about the people who plant and care for them. Tree planting is a community-building activity that brings people together from all walks of life. It fosters a sense of shared purpose and connection to the natural world.

It also provides an opportunity for education and learning, as people of all ages discover the wonders of trees and their importance in our lives.

The benefits of tree planting extend far beyond the environment. Studies have shown that spending time in nature, particularly among trees, can reduce stress, lower blood pressure, boost the immune system, and improve mood and cognitive function. Trees can also enhance the aesthetic appeal of our communities, making them more attractive and livable.

In a world that is increasingly urbanized and disconnected from nature, the symphony of green offers a much-needed antidote. It reminds us of our interconnectedness with the natural world and the importance of preserving our planet for future generations. It also provides us with a sense of hope and renewal, a reminder that even small actions can make a big difference.

Let us all join together to create a symphony of green, a harmonious chorus of trees that will revitalize our planet and enrich our lives.

Let us plant trees in our yards, our parks, and our communities. Let us teach our children to love and appreciate trees, and let us work together to protect our forests for generations to come.

For in the words of the poet, "Until you dig a hole, you plant a tree, you water it and make it survive, you haven't done a thing. You are just talking." Let us act now, let us plant the seeds of change, and let the symphony of green begin.

ᐅᐅᐅ

"The joy of growing is a universal language, spoken
by the rustling leaves, the blooming flowers, and
the soaring birds. Let us learn this language and
join the chorus of nature."

TWENTY-FOUR
SUMMARY

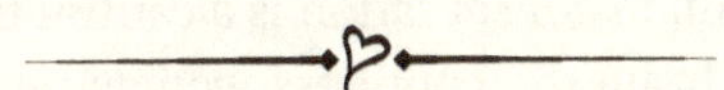

In "Growing a Greener Tomorrow: A Guide to Tree Planting & Conservation," we embark on a journey of ecological empowerment, exploring the profound impact of trees on our lives and the planet. This journey celebrates the unique connection women share with the natural world, highlighting their pivotal role in conservation and sustainable practices.

The book opens with a clarion call to action, urging women to embrace their inner arborist and become champions for trees. We delve into the myriad benefits trees offer, from mitigating climate change and fostering biodiversity to improving air and water quality and enhancing human well-being. It's a reminder that planting a tree is not merely an act of beautification but a tangible contribution to the health and resilience of our planet.

The guide provides practical advice on selecting the right tree for the right place, emphasizing the importance of native species that are well-adapted to local conditions. We learn the art of planting, nurturing, and caring for trees, from preparing the planting site and ensuring proper watering and mulching to pruning and protecting against pests and diseases.

Beyond the technical aspects, "Growing a Greener Tomorrow" delves into the deeper wisdom that trees impart. They teach us patience, resilience, and the interconnectedness of all living things. They inspire us with their strength, beauty, and unwavering commitment to growth. This guide encourages us to connect with trees on a spiritual level, embracing practices such as tree hugging, meditation, and communication, to unlock their hidden wisdom and tap into our own inner strength.

Women's leadership in conservation is a central theme throughout the book. We celebrate the countless women who have dedicated their lives to protecting forests, restoring degraded lands, and promoting sustainable practices. Their stories inspire us, demonstrating the power of grassroots action, community engagement, and female empowerment in driving positive change.

"Growing a Greener Tomorrow" emphasizes the importance of community-based approaches to conservation. It highlights the transformative power of tree planting in building stronger, healthier, and more resilient communities. We learn how trees can create a sense of place and belonging, mitigate the urban heat island effect, reduce air pollution, and provide habitat for wildlife.

The book also delves into the unique challenges and opportunities faced by women in the field of forestry. It celebrates the contributions of women foresters, who bring a holistic and nurturing approach to forest management, emphasizing the importance of biodiversity, soil health, and water quality. The guide provides practical advice for women who aspire to careers in forestry, highlighting the importance of education, mentorship, and networking.

The journey culminates in a celebration of the joy of growing, a testament to the profound relationship between women and trees. It is a reminder that planting a tree is not just an act of environmental responsibility but also a gift to future generations, a symbol of hope, and a legacy of love for the earth.

In conclusion, "Growing a Greener Tomorrow: A Guide to Tree Planting & Conservation" is more than just a practical guide; it is a celebration of the human spirit, a call to action, and a testament to the power of women to create a more sustainable and equitable future for all. It reminds us that by planting trees, we are not only nurturing nature but also nurturing ourselves, our communities, and the planet we call home.

ppp

Citation And References

This book represents the culmination of extensive research and meticulous analysis, incorporating a diverse range of sources, including numerous books, scholarly studies, and personal experiences. Additionally, I have scoured various websites to gather relevant information and data essential for the compilation of this work. I have taken every precaution to ensure the accuracy of the information presented and have diligently cited all sources to acknowledge their contributions.

Despite these efforts, the possibility of inadvertent errors remains. I deeply value the insights of my readers and appreciate any feedback that can help identify and rectify such inaccuracies. I encourage you to bring any discrepancies to my attention.

Your feedback is not only welcome but crucial, as it will aid in correcting current editions and enhancing the content of future ones. I am committed to maintaining the highest standards of accuracy and reliability in my work and thank you for your support and understanding.

Additionally, I firmly uphold the principle of freedom of speech and expression as guaranteed under Article 19(1)(a) of the Constitution of India, and I respect the diverse viewpoints and expressions of all readers.

ϷϷϷ

Other Books Of The Author

1. Empowering Minds: A Journey into Women's Self-Discovery and Power
2. The Dynamics of Motivation: Catalyzing Thought into Action
3. Meditation and Mental Well Being: The Path to Inner Peace and Clarity
4. The Psychology of Child Education: Nurturing Future Generations
5. Ethical Enlightenment: A Modern Guide to Living with Integrity
6. Voices of Empowerment: Stories of Women Rising Against Odds
7. Social Psychology in Everyday Life: Understanding Human Connections
8. The Essence of Motivational Speaking: Inspiring Change in Others
9. Balancing Acts: Women, Work, and the Will to Lead
10. Guiding with Grace: Raising Children with Compassion and Awareness
11. The Power of Positive Aging: Embracing Life After Fifty
12. Building Resilient Communities: Social Work in Action
13. The Ethical Educator: Principles for Teaching and Learning
14. From Insight to Impact: Social Psychology for a Better World
15. The Ethics of Empathy: A Guide to Ethical Living
16. The Science of Empowering the Self: Navigating Life's Challenges with Psychological Wisdom
17. The Mindful Conscious Leader: Meditation Techniques for Modern Management
18. Pioneering Spirit: Women's Pathways to Leadership and Empowerment
19. Feeling to Healing: The Role of Emotional Intelligence in Child Development
20. Transformative Talks and Words of Inspiration: Insights into Motivational Oratory

21. Green Ethics: A Path to Sustainable Living
22. Spiritual Integrity: Navigating Life with Moral Compassion
23. Clean Living, Clean Society: The Ethics of Cleanliness
24. Patriotic Spirits: Building a Nation on Positive Attitudes
25. Innovative Integrity & Vibrant Visions: The Ethical and Entrepreneurial Spirit of Gujarat
26. Youthful Visions, Endless Possibilities: Inspiring Ethics and Motivation in Children
27. Living Your Legacy: How to Motivate Others by Living Your Values
28. Secret of Healing Conversations: Ethical Practices in Counselling and Therapy
29. Creative Kindness: Crafting a Life of Compassion and Creativity
30. The Power of Appreciation: How Gratitude Can Transform Your Relationships
31. Bhagavad-Gita: Messages
32. Science of Art: The New Frontier of Fashion Modernism
33. Vivekananda's Virtues: A Blueprint for Modern Living
34. Empower Her: Navigating the Path to Women's Entrepreneurship
35. The Boundless Classroom: Innovations in Global Education
36. The Language of Leadership: Communicating with Authenticity and Impact
37. The Warrior's Mantra: Deciphering the Hanuman Chalisa
38. Echoes of Empathy: Transformative Stories of Social Service
39. Artful Living: Cultivating Creativity in Your Daily Routine
40. Finding Your Why: Discovering Your Passions and Charting Your Course
41. The Role of Social Media in Shaping Self-Esteem and Interpersonal Relationships among Adolescents
42. Karma's Tapestry: Weaving a Life of Selfless Service
43. Altruistic Alchemy: Transforming Lives Through Giving
44. The Blueprint of Pro-Activeness and Productivity: Crafting Habits for Success
45. The Simplicity with Grounded Wisdom: Embracing Authenticity

in a Complex World

46. Secret of Solopreneur's Odyssey: Navigating the Path to Self-Employment

47. Exploring Tapestry of Peace: Global Perspectives on Harmony

48. The Art and Actions of Connection: Mastering Communication for Impact

49. She Governs and at the Helm: Strategies for Political Empowerment

50. Rising Above and Rising with Grace: A Woman's Roadmap to Career Mastery

51. The Effect of Networking & Connectedness: Building Strategic Alliances for Women

52. Beyond his Barriers: Women Thriving in Male-Dominated Fields

53. Secret of Inner Compass: Navigating Life with Intuition

54. Creative & Pro-Active Muses: A Celebration of Women in the Arts

55. Unburdened: The Art of Releasing the Past

56. Amplified Voices: Speeches of Women that Astonished the World

57. Secret of Manifesting Dreams: A Woman's Guide to Intentional Living

58. Ethics and Value Based Education: Reimagining Japan's School System

59. The Moral Compass Curriculum: A Holistic Approach

60. Tech with Heart: Integrating Ethics into Digital Learning

61. Honoring Virtue: Recognizing Ethical Excellence in Education

62. Raising Good Humans: A Guide to Character Development

63. The Spark Within: Nurturing Creativity in Children

64. The Teenager Whisperer: Navigating Adolescence with Grace

65. Igniting a Passion for Learning: Inspiring Lifelong Curiosity

66. The Habit Lab: Cultivating Positive Behaviors in Children

67. Seeds of Empathy: Fostering Compassion in Young Hearts

68. The Reading Revolution: Inspiring a Love of Books in Children

69. The Learning Brain: Unlocking the Secrets of Student Success

70. Teaching for All: Differentiated Instruction Strategies

71. The Time Alchemist: Mastering Time Management for Peak Performance

72. The Resilience Factor: Transforming Setbacks into Stepping Stones
73. The Healing Touch of Nature: An Introduction to Naturopathy
74. Echoes of the Past: Healing Through Past Life Regression
75. The Spiritual Healer's Handbook: Exploring Energy Medicine
76. Crystal Clarity: Unveiling the Power of Gemstones
77. The Dream Weaver's Guide: Decoding the Language of Dreams
78. Emotional Alchemy: Transforming Pain into Power
79. Sonic Serenity: Harnessing Sound for Stress Relief
80. The Entrepreneur's Playbook: Launching Your Business with Confidence
81. Productivity Unleashed: Time Management Strategies for Entrepreneurs
82. The Problem Solver's Toolkit: Creative Solutions for Business Challenges
83. The Future is Now: Emerging Trends in Business
84. The Curious Explorer: A Child's Guide to Scientific Discovery
85. Digital Pioneers: Empowering Kids in the Tech World
86. The Young Philosopher's Guide: Exploring Life's Big Questions
87. Finding Your Voice: Communication Skills for Confident Kids
88. Nature's Playground: A Child's Guide to Outdoor Adventure
89. Growing a Greener Tomorrow: A Guide to Tree Planting & Conservation
90. Driving with Purpose: Ethical Choices on the Road
91. The Healing Touch: Cultivating Compassion in Healthcare
92. Navigating the Digital Landscape: Ethics in the Age of Social Media
93. The Ethical Closet: A Guide to Sustainable Fashion
94. The Mindful Voyager: Sustainable Travel Practices
95. The Feminine Divine: Honoring the Goddesses of India
96. Sacred Sounds: Chanting Your Way to Inner Peace
97. The Yoga Path: Uniting with the Divine Within
98. Rites of Passage: Creating Meaningful Ceremonies
99. The Chakra System: A Map of Inner Transformation
100. Spiritual Sangha: Finding Community through Satsang and

Bhajan
101. Pilgrimage of the Soul: Spiritual Journeys in India

❧❧❧

Contact

Dr. Minakshi Bansal
Social Activist
Ahmedabad, Gujarat, Bharat
minakshiindiag20@yahoo.com

❥❥❥

|| LOKAHA SAMASTHAHA SUKHINO BHAVANTU ||